NEFERTITI

PHILIPP
VANDENBERG

Also by Philipp Vandenberg
THE CURSE OF THE PHARAOHS
translated by Thomas Weyr

NEFERTITI

AN ARCHAEOLOGICAL BIOGRAPHY

translated
from the German
by Ruth Hein

HODDER AND STOUGHTON
LONDON   SYDNEY   AUCKLAND   TORONTO

The photographs following page 66 of the bust of Nefertiti and the head of Tiy are from Bildarchiv Preussischer Kulturbesitz; that of the head of Amunhotep III is from The Brooklyn Museum, Charles Edwin Wilbour Fund.

The photographs following page 130, with the exception of the limestone relief from the great palace of Akhetaten, are from Hirmer Fotoarchiv Munchen.

Vandenberg, Philipp
  Nefertiti.
  1. Nefertiti, *Queen of Egypt*
  2. Egypt – Queens – Biography
  I. Hein, Ruth
  932'.01'0924   DT87.45

ISBN 0-340-23408-3

CONTENTS

PROLOGUE   9

1 | THE FIND   17
2 | THE PHARAOH   27
3 | THE METROPOLIS   40
4 | DEATH OF A PHARAOH   62
5 | THE SUCCESSOR   79
6 | THE CITY OF DREAMS   95
7 | THE DISCORD   124
8 | THE END   134

EPILOGUE   151

APPENDIXES   155

    A Partial Chronology of
      the New Kingdom
    B Nefertiti's Family
      Relationships
    C Chronology of Nefertiti's
      Life
    D The Egyptian Calendar

SUGGESTED READING   160

Photograph sections follow pages 66 and 130.

PROLOGUE

The year was 1842. Although the German Egyptologist Richard Lepsius was only thirty-two years old, he assumed the leadership of an archaeological expedition to the Nile River Valley of Egypt. It was said that somewhere in the region of Amarna—halfway between the old capital of Memphis and the new capital of Thebes—had once stood a royal city, glittering with gold, which eventually sank into the desert. No one knew the name of the city, its significance, or how long it had endured.

Others before Lepsius had found jewelry, vessels, and tombs with relief-carved walls in the area, but Lepsius was the first to discover *her*—a woman described with admiration on every monument found in the rocky desert or dug up out of the sand: "The beautiful and magnificent one with the feathered crown; the great crown princess in the palace; great in gladness, we rejoice when we hear her voice; mistress of loveliness; great in popularity; the woman whose being gladdens the lord of both lands [Upper and Lower Egypt]; his beloved great royal wife; the mistress of both lands; the beloved of fortune; beautiful is the beauty of the sun; the beautiful one who is come, may she live forever."

Lepsius did not really know what to make of these epithets, which he had found on the rock walls, on stone blocks, and in the vaults. Clearly all of them—eighteen altogether—referred to a queen who had been indescribably beautiful and indescribably popular. Perhaps she had even been a pharaoh in her own right. But the texts also spoke of a "lord of both lands; the sole one or Re; he who lives by the truth; beautiful are the shapes of Re, beloved of the Aten"—without a doubt also a pharaoh.

"The beautiful one who is come" is the ancient Egyptian meaning of Nefertiti, and such was clearly the woman's name. And the other pharaoh must have been called "beautiful are the shapes of Re" (Neferkheperure) or "the sole one of Re" (Uaenre).

However, in spite of these great discoveries, an immense problem was created. For the list of kings and dynasties compiled by the Egyptian priest Manetho of Sebennytos around the year 200 B.C., which supposedly contained every pharaonic name from the first to the thirty-first dynasty, mentioned no one whom any of these names would even remotely fit. In any case, Lepsius was unable to identify the woman, and she remained a legend for over fifty years—the subject of "the case of Nefertiti."

Two generations of archaeologists struggled with greater or lesser success to solve the riddle posed by Nefertiti from

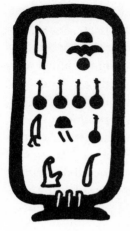 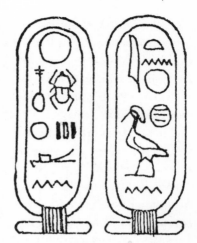

Name cartouches of Nefertiti (left) and Akhenaten (Amunhotep IV). Nefertiti's reads: Beautiful is the beauty of the Aten, the Beautiful One who is come. Akhenaten's: Complete in appearances is Re, the sole one of Re, perfect for the Aten.

the moment of her rediscovery. Around the turn of the century one of these Egyptologists, Norman de Garis Davies, copied the inscriptions on the boundary blocks with which the mysterious king and his enigmatic consort had marked the borders of their city. On these stones—so-called stelae— the same royal couple was depicted together with two, three, four, or six children. The stela texts reveal that the couple had erected the city to honor the god Aten, the glowing disk of the sun. The pharaoh had called himself Akhenaten, his beautiful wife was called Nefertiti, and their city was called Akhetaten.

Scholars developed various bold theories, inventing "careers" from foundling to female pharaoh. Others speculated that Akhenaten was a woman disguised as a man. Or might

Nefertiti be that daughter of the Egyptian pharaoh who had found Moses in the bulrushes after he had been abandoned in a willow basket on the Nile? Such eminent Egyptologists as Auguste Mariette thought that the Akhenaten allied with Nefertiti was a eunuch—someone captured in a Sudanese campaign and deprived of his manhood.

These speculations were not simply products of the imagination, for the man identified in numerous inscriptions as Nefertiti's royal consort and ruler of Upper and Lower Egypt was often depicted with pronouncedly female features. Like Nefertiti, he had swelling breasts and a narrow waist; unlike her, he had heavy thighs and thin calves. In short, his was a ridiculously repulsive appearance—a distinct contrast to the "mistress of loveliness."

In the meantime archaeologists all over the world worked on the "case." With the zeal of detectives they assembled stone after stone and reconstructed the foundations of an epoch in Egyptian history the significance of which Egyptologists had not previously perceived.

But their work was made more difficult by a strange phenomenon. Wherever the name of Nefertiti or her supposed consort, Akhenaten, appeared or should have appeared in the texts, there were often gaps—the names were scratched out, painted over, or chipped away. In most pictures the woman's head had also been rendered unrecognizable.

It soon became apparent that there was a method behind this madness. Clearly enemies of Nefertiti had attempted to extinguish her memory by an act of iconoclasm. Nevertheless, they had been only partly successful. Furthermore, though a royal tomb was found to have been hollowed out of the rock for Nefertiti and Akhenaten, it had remained incomplete; when it was found, it contained some funerary furnishings but neither the mummy of Nefertiti nor that of her husband.

Though the experts were regularly baffled by such findings, the indefatigable thirst for knowledge of American, British, German, and French archaeologists eventually determined that Nefertiti had been the royal consort of a pharaoh who went unmentioned in the lists of kings. In these lists Amunhotep III's name was followed directly by that of the soldier-pharaoh Horemheb. A period of thirty years—during which no less than four pharaohs held sway—had simply been omitted by the historians of antiquity (see Appendix A).

One of the kings passed over by ancient historical records was Amunhotep IV, the son of Amunhotep III and his wife Tiy. Amunhotep IV had lived in the fourteenth century B.C. and had married a woman whose origins were unknown but whose beauty was praised by all—Nefertiti. In the sixth year of his reign the pharaoh and his queen had moved into a city they had erected for themselves and their followers halfway between Memphis and Thebes. The city bore the name Akhetaten, "horizon of the Aten," and was dedicated to the god Aten, the disk of the sun, which the young ruling couple came to recognize as the *only* god. Within a very few years the old gods, under their supreme divinity Amun, were dethroned and an end was made to the rule of the Amun priests. As a sign of his religious reformation movement, Amunhotep IV changed his name, calling himself Akhenaten, "pleasing to the Aten" or "serviceable to the Aten." Nefertiti seemed to have had considerable influence on the new monotheistic faith.

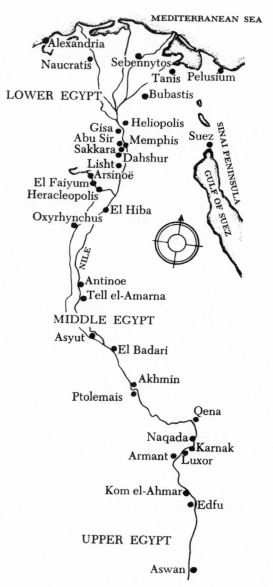

The ancient Egypt of the pharaohs. All the historic sites are located directly on the Nile or only a few miles from this lifeline.

Akhenaten died at the age of thirty or so. Nefertiti did not live on much longer. After her death the pharaohs returned to traditional polytheism and attempted to expunge the names and likenesses of the two "heretics."

Though Akhenaten's genealogy was known by 1900, Nefertiti's ancestry was still shrouded in obscurity and mystery. Who was she in reality? Was she a daughter of Amunhotep III, and did she assume the legitimate succession to the throne through marriage with her own brother Amunhotep IV, who called himself Akhenaten? Or was she the issue of one of the many hundreds of relationships maintained by Amunhotep III? Was she the daughter of one of those 127 Asiatic princes whom Amunhotep II brought back in chains from his raids in Canaan and Syria? Was she a slave who owed her freedom to her beauty? Or was she the daughter of a respectable Theban family?

As the most recent findings indicate, Nefertiti was in all likelihood an Asiatic princess whose father bartered her to the pharaoh Amunhotep III for pure gold. Her life was one long adventure that touched the heights and depths of human destiny. She lived both in unspeakable wealth and also in the most bitter loneliness. She was beloved to the point of idolatry, but she was also unfathomably hated. She was affable and proud, happy and desperate, devoted and cold—a fascinating woman.

At the age of seventeen she was widowed for the first time; when she was thirty, her second husband, whose mental powers had failed, bestowed his favors on another man, who at that time was married to one of Nefertiti's daughters.

Nefertiti gave birth to six daughters. The oldest stole her glory; the second died in childhood; the third had a fate similar to her mother's except that she was only fifteen years old when she died; we know very little of the other three.

At the age of thirty-seven or thereabouts this beautiful woman died in absolute solitude. Hardly a soul took notice of her death, so that historians today have difficulty in determining the year it happened. And yet there was a time when she was the idol of a whole generation—and not only because of her beauty, proclaimed by countless inscriptions.

The true extent of her radiance was discovered in 1912 by a handful of German archaeologists in Amarna, Egypt.

Were I to describe this find the way it happened, with its confusion, its expectations, its minor setbacks, the reader would be as perplexed as we were at the time.

—*Ludwig Borchardt*

1 / ·THE FIND

December 6, 1912. Amarna, Egypt, site of the ancient city of Akhetaten.

A group of archaeologists from the German Orient Society, headed by Professor Ludwig Borchardt of Berlin, had divided the ruined city of the sun into grids. Each section measured six hundred square feet and was identified by a letter and a number.

Today the archaeologists were concentrating their work on Grid Square P 47, since finds from the previous season indicated they had uncovered a district where, three thousand years earlier, builders, artisans, and artists had plied their trade. On the very first day of the new season—November 25, 1912—the diggers had brought to light a miniature group of figures made of limestone. The artifact, discovered between the walls of an as yet unidentified complex of buildings, was easily recognizable as an unfinished

17

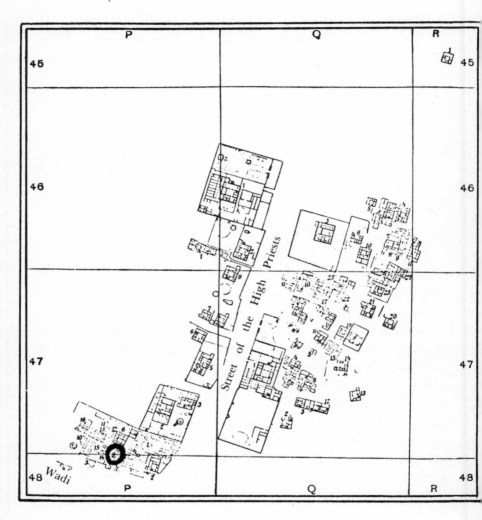

Map of the excavations of 1912–13. The circle (bottom left) marks the place where the bust of Nefertiti was found.

sculpture representing a pharaoh holding his child on his knees and kissing him.

Professor Hermann Ranke, who was in charge of the digging on December 6, was hoping for new finds to confirm the archaeologists' belief that they had discovered the workshop of a sculptor. Several more heads and busts had already come to light in these chambers, making the hope a realistic one. Furthermore, in Grid Square P 47 huge rubbish dumps had been found that contained rock splinters of several different kinds—the sort that would pile up in a large sculptor's workshop. These shards could not be refuse from demolished buildings, since in ancient Egypt such structures were always made of a single kind of stone.

By pure chance the archaeologists had also stumbled upon a find that, seemingly insignificant at first, was soon to prove outstanding. The artifact was a portion of an ivory lid with an inscription indicating that it had belonged to Thutmose, a master sculptor and the most prominent of the thousands of artists and artisans who had shaped Akhetaten, the first planned city in the world.

Shortly after one o'clock in the afternoon a young Egyptian hired to help in the digs came running to the ramshackle hut where the diggers stored their tools and the scientists kept their materials. "Mister, mister!" he shouted while he was still at some distance.

The "mister" who stepped out into the scorching sun was Ludwig Borchardt. This was his second year as head of the Amarna digs. Visibly excited, the Egyptian waved a note from Professor Ranke. Hastily scribbled in pencil, it read, *Urgent! Life-size painted bust in P 47!*

"I'm coming," Borchardt said to the messenger, who was still standing before him. "I'm coming," he repeated.

The boy understood at last and ran back. Borchardt, as if under the spell of premonition, followed somewhat more slowly.

Arrived in P 47, Borchardt made his way across dust and stones into the narrow chamber (Room 19), only six feet wide and thirty-five feet long, where Mohammed, the foreman, had come across the unusual find while clearing away a three-foot layer of debris. Across the room from the door, in the left-hand corner, Borchardt caught sight of the neck of a woman, flesh-colored with painted red bands.

He used his hands to sweep aside the rubble, and soon the join of the head appeared. Irritated, he stopped briefly when the back of the head began to sprout into an immense shape, but finally he recognized the outlines of a queen's headdress such as was worn by only one other person—Tiy, the principal wife of Amunhotep III.

The bust's features were still concealed, for the sculpture lay buried in the debris head down and with its face turned to the wall. Many minutes passed before the chin, the nose, the full face appeared. Then Borchardt, Ranke, and Mohammed carefully lifted the twenty-inch-high find from the dust. They were holding the head of a queen—one whose timelessly beautiful features were to become the best known in history.

This priceless work of art was preserved almost undamaged. Both ears were lightly chipped, and the insert of the left eye was missing. Borchardt immediately gave orders to sift all the rubble from Room 19, including even those sackfuls that had already been taken away. The debris amounted to about thirty cubic feet—two medium-sized truckloads. The job occupied two full days and resembled the proverbial search for a needle in a haystack. The complicated job, however, was to culminate in only partial success. Though fragments of the ears were found, the paste insert for the left eye remained lost. "Only much later did I realize," Ludwig Borchardt wrote in his findings report, "that it had never existed."

At no other time has a human eye aroused so much speculation and excitement. Why would a work of art perfected down to the smallest detail lack an eye?

Borchardt advanced the theory that Thutmose had deliberately omitted the left eye to demonstrate to his students how the material must be worked in order to insert it. But this theory must be considered suspect, since the eye socket gives no indication of ever having been worked on.

Today, many Egyptologists concur in the belief that the world-famous bust represents Nefertiti at about age twenty-five. (Others theorize it represents her daughter Meritaten.) Could the beautiful queen have lost her left eye sometime before that age? After all, diseases of the eye were no less rare in ancient Egypt than they are in the land of the Nile today. Unfortunately, this theory is contradicted by a number of other finds. Numerous wall reliefs and three-dimensional sculptures have been discovered that depict Nefertiti at earlier and later ages, and none of them exhibits a damaged left eye.

Another theory proposed by Egyptologists is that the bust was simply left unfinished. This idea is somewhat strengthened by the fact that the inhabitants of Akhetaten abandoned the city literally almost overnight. But even this theory must fall by the wayside, since at the time Akhetaten was given up, Nefertiti was at least thirty-five years old.

The most recent scholarly findings seem to point to a possible solution of the problem. As we know today, Akhenaten, whom Nefertiti married when she was eighteen, was disabled at an early age by severe sexual dysfunction. Thus, although Nefertiti had six daughters, Akhenaten can be regarded with certainty as the father of only the first three. New finds, such as the three tablets of the "courtroom reports" of Amarna (1970), also confirm that Nefertiti was not averse to a little straying now and then but that she dropped her lovers without further ado when she tired of them. Thus it seems reasonable to ask whether Nefertiti might have fallen in love with Thutmose when she served as his model. Perhaps even as he worked on the bust, Thutmose himself lost his heart to the beautiful queen, who, as he must have known, had already conferred her favors on numerous men.

In fact the bust of Nefertiti emits a fascinating, almost erotic radiance, as Borchardt confirmed by his spontaneous entry in the finding report: "We hold in our hands the Egyptian work of art that is most strongly imbued with life." But it seems that Thutmose suffered the same fate as so many others before him. Nefertiti, the beautiful one, beckoned. Perhaps she did much more—only to reject the disappointed lover, who had no avenue of revenge. And perhaps he retaliated in the only way open to him—he did not mutilate his work of art, the image of his love; he punished with incompleteness.

Only a yard away from the bust of Nefertiti, Borchardt pulled from the debris the shards of a bust of Akhenaten.

The fact that the sculpture was broken hints at a burst of anger on the part of the sculptor. It is unlikely that Theban iconoclasts are responsible for the demolition; they would surely have destroyed Nefertiti's likeness as well. After all, she was the driving force behind the heretic Aten religion.

Why was Nefertiti's bust so well preserved? Reconstructions have revealed that the busts of Akhenaten and Nefertiti had stood on a wooden shelf in the little chamber that adjoined Thutmose's living hall to the east. But while the sculpture of Akhenaten had been pushed off the ledge during the flowering of the sun city of Akhetaten and had splintered on the smooth stone floor, the image of Nefertiti had remained untouched for at least several decades on the ledge, standing there until the board rotted or was gnawed to pieces by the termites that are quite common in Egypt.

By the time the insects had done their work, the onetime capital of the Egyptian empire had long since been abandoned by its inhabitants. The Nile mud used to cement the building stone had loosened in the masonry; the hot wind had driven the dirty-gray sand of the desert into the empty, gaping buildings. Then—at some moment or other—the weathered wooden shelf gave way under Nefertiti's bust, the statue's heavy skull unbalanced the weight, and the bust fell into the sand, the flat surface of the wig downward, the sensitive face and fragile neck pointing upward. The decades that followed scattered more dusty mud and sand onto the ruins.

Borchardt and Ranke did not immediately recognize what they had discovered. The only aspect that was clear from the outset was that the beautiful woman whose image they beheld was a queen. Her rank was shown by the tall headdress, painted blue at the hairline, which was to indicate that the queen, like every divine being, had hair of lapis lazuli. Presumably, however, by evening of the day of the find Borchardt had already become certain of the identity of this female head. As he admitted later on, he was sitting over his diary until long after midnight—quite contrary to his custom—trying to describe the find enthusiastically down to the smallest detail. But after a few pages, overwhelmed by what had happened, he gave up with the emphatic notation, "Description is no use; observation!"

It might be supposed that Borchardt, having unearthed the most valuable object in Egyptian art to that time, would have let the world know about it as soon as possible. But nothing of the sort happened. In fact, it was not until 1920, when the bust suddenly surfaced in the Berlin Museum, that the story was published. To this day it is still not absolutely clear how Nefertiti made her way to Germany.

The Egyptian authorities had given permission for Borchardt's excavations on condition that all finds be divided equally between the National Museum in Cairo and the Berlin Museum. Only duplicates and pieces of inferior quality were to be taken out of the country by the German excavators, and even that provision was contingent on the approval of the National Museum's Department of Antiquities, headed by Gaston Maspero.

Borchardt insisted that on January 20, 1913, he had come to an agreement with Maspero to the effect that Berlin was to receive Nefertiti while Cairo was to receive an altarpiece discovered somewhat earlier. However, according to Egyptian authorities, what really happened is that

Borchardt wrote to Gaston Maspero a few days after his discovery, asking the curator to come to Amarna to examine the finds. None of them, he assured Maspero, was remarkable, but there were a few trifles that he would like to send to Berlin for study purposes. On the basis of the letter, Maspero felt that his personal presence was unnecessary and dispatched an assistant. The young man, in turn, picked up the finds, listing them in his report as "a few baskets of clay shards and many sandstone fragments." The young inspector found no objects that were suitable for exhibition at the Cairo museum. Without checking back with his superior, he signed the papers required for exportation. Soon thereafter five crates were shipped to Alexandria. One of those wooden boxes must have contained something other than the limestone fragments and clay shards declared on the manifest.

When Nefertiti emerged in Berlin, all tracks were covered. And this mystery is the real reason the bust was kept under wraps for so long. The Egyptian authorities formally inquired in Berlin where this unique find had originated and how it had found its way to Berlin. The answer was that the acquisition had followed the regular procedure, with official approval of the Egyptian Department of Antiquities. Attempts were made in Cairo to reconstruct the case, now several years old, and the Egyptian government demanded the return of the bust. Since all diplomatic contacts were to no avail, the Department of Antiquities in Cairo posed an ultimatum—either the bust of Nefertiti was returned, or no German archaeologist would ever again be allowed to sink his spade into Egyptian soil.

For years German Egyptologists were personae non

gratae in Egypt, and to this day other foreign archaeologists are not allowed to export any of their finds. As a
result, the National Museum in Cairo is bursting at the
seams with art treasures, becoming more and more a vast
storehouse of nightmarish proportions. But who can blame
the Egyptians for their reaction?

It seems that the discovery of Nefertiti took the same
course as did her life, three thousand years earlier: roman-
tic and unique.

One of the most interesting conclusions, of great importance to Egyptologists, is that the pharaohs as a whole form an extremely heterogeneous group. Indeed, if it were not known that all of these mummies were of Egyptian kings, if they had been found in different parts of the world, no one would have thought there was any relationship among them.

—James E. Harris

2 / THE PHARAOH

December 1966. Shortly after nine o'clock in the morning James E. Harris, a geneticist and anthropologist at the University of Michigan, and Kent R. Weeks, an Egyptologist at Cairo University, arrived at the National Museum in Cairo. The two Americans had been given permission by the Egyptian authorities to X-ray the royal mummies—twenty pharaohs and seven queens—preserved there in hermetically sealed glass sarcophagi. The scholars were primarily concerned with diagnosing genetic developments and possible causes of death—a fascinating project, but technically quite complicated. The X-ray unit was set up in a room adjoining the chamber where the mummies were displayed, and each mummy had to be taken out of its glass coffin and carried to the X-ray unit separately. Speaking of the chore, Harris reported, "Too much moving, too sudden a jolt, and the mummy's skin might crumble or a

27

bone snap, and it often took the steady hands of four men half an hour to position the body."

The X-rays—six to eight of each mummy—were exposed for three to five minutes. Then the film was rushed to a nearby hotel, where the scientists had set up a makeshift darkroom in a bathroom. Only when they were certain that the pictures were really perfect was the mummy taken from the X-ray table and returned to its glass sarcophagus. The undertaking, which extended over four years, was a great scientific success.

One of the most pitiful mummies the American scholars laid out on the X-ray table was thought to be the mortal remains of the pharaoh Amunhotep III. The third Amunhotep, who had been discovered in the tomb of his grandfather, Amunhotep II, consisted of disjointed parts. The arms and legs had been separated from the trunk. Nevertheless they looked astonishingly alive, since, as the X-rays revealed, the embalmers had packed the arms and legs with linen cloths soaked in resin. Through the passage of time the limbs had attained a degree of such hardness that the linen pads even screened out X rays.

The pathological examination of the mummy of Amunhotep III brought the following findings. The pharaoh had died somewhere around fifty years of age. Fat, with a bald pate and a toothless mouth studded with alveolar abscesses, he cannot have been a delectable sight during the final years of his life.

This was the man Nefertiti was compelled to marry when she was fifteen years old.

Amunhotep III was only twelve years old—fifteen at most—when he took over the throne of Egypt from his father,

Thutmose IV, who had died young. His mother, Mutemwiya, was a daughter of King Shuttarna of Mitanni, a
powerful and influential Asian kingdom in northern
Mesopotamia.

Nebmaatre (Amunhotep's regnal name) had received an
extremely attractive girl in marriage at the time he ascended
the throne: Tiy, the eleven- or twelve-year-old daughter of
the priest Yuya and the royal harem lady (some Egyptologists even consider her a princess) Tuya. Never before in
Egyptian history were the parents of a pharoah's wife proclaimed in a manner comparable to that accorded Yuya and
Tuya. Yuya was given the title God's Father, which meant
"father of the pharaoh." Tuya was named Mistress of the
Harem of Amun—that is, high priestess.

A portrait bust of Tiy as a mature woman, worked in
ebony inlay and preserved in the Berlin Museum, shows the
features of a person of unusual self-assurance. It did not
bother her that her husband married concubines at least a
dozen times and that his harem comprised several hundred
beautiful women. These girls came and went without in any
way jeopardizing her influential position at the court of the
pharaoh. She received the titles Principal Heir and Princess
of All Women, Princess of the Two Lands [Upper and Lower
Egypt], and Princess of the South and the North.

The state treasury was bulging with tributes from vassals
to the north and south when Amunhotep began his rule.
But since the pharaoh was more interested in his own pleasures than in ruling, he spent the riches of the state primarily on luxuries. He ate from golden plates; he loved wine,
women, and song; and he arranged numerous hunting
parties and festivals. His mortuary temple on the eastern

Amunhotep III and some priests pull on ropes in order to raise the Djer pillar, a ceremony that was carried out at dusk before the onset of winter. To the right the king is seen making an offering to Djer in a chapel. The Djer pillar is related to a fetish—perhaps a felled tree trunk or a papyrus bundle— tracing back to local fertility cults of prehistoric times. (Drawing copied from a relief in the tomb of Kheriuf in Thebes, chief steward of Queen Tiy.)

bank of the Nile was one of the largest and most opulent memorial buildings in all of ancient Egypt. The approach avenue was flanked by stone jackals and watched over by two mighty colossi, seated figures each as tall as a six-story building, weighing 720 tons and chiseled from a single block of stone. By analyzing the mineral content of these mammoth stones, physicists in 1974 proved that they must have been hauled to the building site from the quarries of

Aswan, a distance of 120 miles. How this was done will probably never be learned.

Amunhotep III, who was called the Magnificent, also had a palace built for himself and his queen near Malkata, on the western bank of the Nile near the capital of Thebes. He intended it to be an object of admiration for the entire world. Although it was the custom in ancient Egypt to erect temples and palaces from rock or Nile-mud bricks, the proud pharaoh chose a quite different and much more costly building material: wood. Three thousand years ago in Egypt, wood was every bit as expensive as it is today. Amunhotep imported cedars from Lebanon. Only the outer walls of the palace, the flooring, and the retaining pillars of the roof were made of stone; the interior walls, the roofs, and the balustrades were wooden.

This light, amusing style of architecture reflected the life style of Amunhotep III. He built for himself, not for eternity; the wooden structure suffered disproportionately to the stone buildings from the effects of weathering, and the more resistant foundations were misused as a quarry by his successors.

The pharaoh had problems on both the political and the religious fronts in his domestic affairs, since politics and religion were tightly intertwined in ancient Egypt. We must remember that, since the eleventh dynasty, the god Amun was considered the highest ranking of all deities, at least in Thebes. Amun was also considered the father of whatever pharaoh happened to be ruling. Thus an increasingly close relationship had developed between the powerful Amun priesthood and the royal house. Eventually the oracle of Amun was determining the successor to the throne and so initiating the course of the whole country's future. Further-

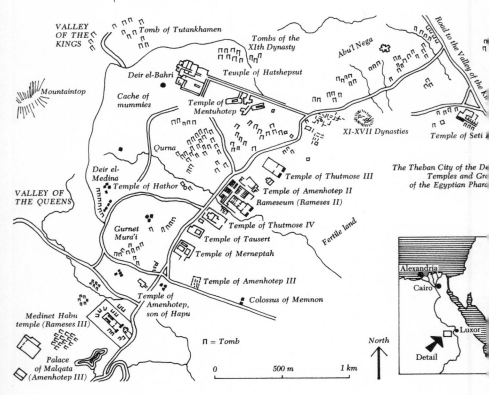

The Theban City of the Dead.

more, the high priest of Amun traditionally held the political office of vizier—second in power only to the pharaoh.

Amunhotep III can hardly be said to have rejected the Amun cult. He carried on the tradition of building "monuments such as had never before been seen" to Amun, and the major Amun festivals continued to be celebrated. Yet there are many indications that under Amunhotep a new, rival cult began to grow—the cult of the Aten.

Originally, Aten was a word without religious significance, standing only for the orb of the sun, the solar disk. But by the fifth year of Amunhotep III's reign—around the year 1397 B.C.—he defeated the rebelling Sudanese tribes "at the command of Amun-Aten." This is the first instance of the equation—even the connection—of Amun and Aten. And soon thereafter, upon the death of his vizier Ptahotep, Amunhotep III installed in the position, not the new high priest of Amun, but an outsider, the noble Ramose.

By erecting his palace at Malkata—which was separated by the Nile from the old Theban palace, the Amun temples, and especially the caste of the Amun priests—Amunhotep III established a clearly visible symbol, admired by the populace.

His personal refuge in this palace was called the "house of Nebmaatre, which is the magnificent splendor of the Aten." By and by the Aten was also encountered on monuments. "Hail to you, O Aten of the day, who awakenest the dead into life, who givest them life"—so reads a hymn that has been eternalized because two architects of Amunhotep III affixed it to a temple wall in Thebes.

A final but no less interesting example of the beginnings of the Aten cult occurred in early August of the year 1391 B.C. Tiy, the "great royal wife," was offended to the quick when the Amun priests neglected to ask her to play the role of the goddess Mut, Amun's wife, during a ceremonial celebration on the holy sea. When she asked the pharaoh to make her a gift of a pleasure lake, so that she would at least be able to amuse herself alone, Amunhotep did not hesitate. He gathered together every one of the 250,000 workmen employed on all the various projects in his huge city.

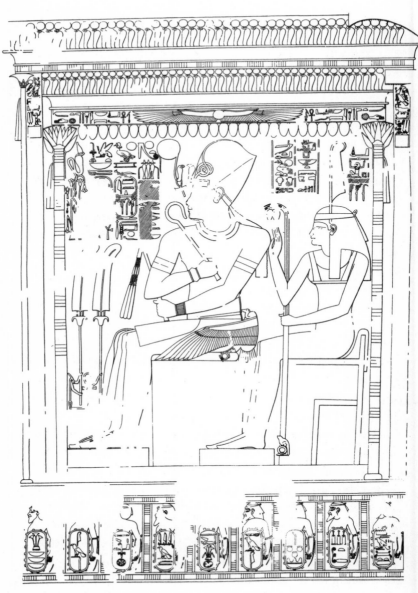

Amunhotep III and Tiy shown enthroned under a canopy. (Part of a scene from the northern portal of the tomb of Kheriuf in Thebes.)

Within two weeks they had excavated an artificial lake east of the Malkata palace, measuring roughly 2,850 yards by 455 yards. Because this incredible process has been meticulously preserved for us on a memorial scarab, there is no doubt about the exact date, the time required for the work, and the extent of the enterprise.

> Year 11, Akhet, Day 1 [The third inundation month, Akhet, lasted from August 15 to September 15], under the majesty of Horus, Strong Bull, Appeared in Truth, of the two mistresses, "who fixes the laws and calms the two lands," the gold Horus, Great in Strength, Who Defeats the Asiatic, King of Upper and Lower Egypt, Nebmaatre, son of Re Amunhotep, ruler of Thebes, long may he live. The great royal wife Tiy, may she live. His majesty commanded that a lake be constructed for the great royal wife Tiy in the city of Djarukha, 3,700 cubits long and 700 cubits wide. His majesty accomplished the feast of the inauguration of the lake on the sixteenth day of 3 Akhet in that his majesty was rowed in the royal barge Splendor of the Aten.

The element of the inscription that concerns us most is the name given to the royal barge—Splendor of the Aten.

In addition to his religious and political problems at home, Amunhotep III also had difficulties in other areas of his far-flung empire. Word had spread all too quickly of the pharaoh's weakness in foreign affairs, and his empire began to crumble at its borders. When his vassals begged for aid, the pharaoh did not respond. When he sent ambassadors to the provinces, he was interested in only one thing: women.

At the time of the eighteenth dynasty relations between the Egyptian pharaohs and the Near Eastern kings were characterized by a lively diplomatic traffic. Thutmose IV had traveled through his Asiatic colonies, but Amunhotep III preferred to keep the Asiatics in check through gold—gold that, we are told over and over again, was as plentiful in Egypt as dust. Egyptian gold traveled northward by the ton to the kings of Mitanni, but the flow was not powered by friendship or generosity. The kings of Mitanni paid for it with their daughters, their sisters, and their aunts—just so long as they were pretty enough.

For three generations the pharaohs of the eighteenth dynasty imported Mitanni princesses complete with retinue—for a hefty price, of course, which the Mitannian kings knew how to drive up steadily through years of backing and filling. As we have already noted, Amunhotep III was the son of the Mitannian princess Mutemwiya, a daughter of King Shuttarna. Tiy may have been from Mitanni; and in the tenth year of Amunhotep's reign, when he was about twenty-five, he had again married a Mitannian—Gilukhipa, another daughter of Shuttarna.

Late in Amunhotep's reign, when he was about fifty, one of King Shuttarna's sons, named Tushratta, ascended the throne of Mitanni. Because of a fascinating group of stone tablets referred to as the Amarna letters, we know a good deal about the correspondence between Tushratta and Amunhotep III. Tushratta had repeatedly but discreetly called Amunhotep's attention to his exceedingly pretty daughter Tadukhipa, though at the time she was still a child. Finally the aging pharaoh accepted Tushratta's offer of his daughter and sent a courier named Mane to Mitanni with the request that King Tushratta send Princess Tadukhipa to Egypt because he, Amunhotep III, wished to wed her.

In his letter of reply to his "dear son-in-law" Tushratta

Commemorative scarabs from the eighteenth dynasty. Amulets in the shape of scarab beetles were generally made of glazed soapstone and were rather small. Left: A "lion hunt" scarab from Year 10 of the reign of Amunhotep III. Right: A large scarab (1.5 inches long) belonging to Thutmose IV in commemoration of gifts from Mitanni which the pharaoh appears to have received on the occasion of his marriage to a Mitannian princess. The writing notes that the Aten lighted the way of the king in battle when he brought alien nations under the lawfulness of the god.

promised the princess, but—he was very emphatic on this point—at the same time he stated that he needed gold, much gold. Amunhotep again sent Mane to Mitanni. Tushratta would have the gold he desired, but first he must send his daughter to Egypt. Instead of Mane, a certain Haramassi returned. Mane had been placed under house arrest by Tushratta because the gifts Amunhotep had sent with the messenger were inferior—so inferior that Tushratta, as he generously admitted, had wept.

To win his messenger's release, the pharaoh sent additional gifts to Mitanni, and thereupon Mane was set free. Scarcely had he arrived back home in Thebes, however, than he had to take the road to Mitanni again—accompanied by an interpreter who was to draft the marriage contract.

Amunhotep was to fulfill the following conditions: border regulation in the north through the exchange of the cities of Harwuhe—to Egypt—and Masrianne—to Mitanni (the two cities were given copies of the contractual document); gold and silver for Tushratta, as much as he needed and several pictures of ivory; and the return by Amunhotep of the gold portrait of Tadukhipa which Tushratta had sent the pharaoh for inspection.

Tushratta, for his part, added to his daughter's dowry choice trinkets and jewelry along with the usual gifts from a father, such as horses, chariots, weapons, beds, chests, clothing, and dishes. "Read the dowry list of Gilukhipa and Shuttarna's sister seven times," Tushratta proudly wrote. "Then you will see that the dowry with which I send my daughter Tadukhipa into marriage is much greater, swifter, and more worthy of a pharaoh."

Tadukhipa knew nothing of this trade. It was 1366 B.C., the thirty-sixth year of the reign of Amunhotep III, and he had barely two more years to live. Tadukhipa was fifteen years old, but even before her festive retinue brought her to Egypt—without her dowry, it must be noted—she must have known that her future husband was gravely ill. For with her there traveled to Thebes a wonder-working statue of the goddess Ishtar of Nineveh.

Amunhotep III hoped that the miraculous statue of Ishtar would ease his terrible toothaches. Bleeding teeth and suppurating gums must have turned the final years of this ruler, who was once so zestful, into a torment. Though Ishtar was more properly the Sumerian and Babylonian-Assyrian goddess of love and war, she apparently also had an unusual power to heal, for during the reign of Tushratta's father she had been sent to Thebes once before and had cured the pharaoh. From a theological point of view, this was a colossal undertaking and a first sign of decay of the Egyptian cultus. We must remember that the Egyptian pharaoh was not only the head of state but also the religious leader—himself a god to be adored.

During the eighteenth dynasty it was unusual for a foreign princess such as Tadukhipa to take on a new name when she adopted a new home. The change may have been made because the exotic name was too much of a tongue twister for the Egyptians or because they were bestowing a special favor on the newcomer. In the case of Princess Tadukhipa, the latter seems to have been the case, for she became known as Nefertiti—"the beautiful one who is come."

*Thebes, city of Egyptians, how rich are the houses
In treasures. Hundreds of gates are there, and from
each
Two hundred strong men move out
To the fight with horses and chariots.*
—Homer, Iliad, *Book Nine*

3 | THE METROPOLIS

It was a lurid sight: a bull, trussed, lay on the great stone sacrificial slab. Its limbs twitched in the glow of the oil flames, burning white, when the high priest of Amun, adorned with a tiara, surrounded by a throng of ecstatic priests, slowly marched toward the animal with a knife clutched in his hand and thrust it into the animal's throat. At once temple acolytes, specifically engaged for this service, began to gut and carve up the bloody, half-dead bull.

As martial sounds of cymbals and rattles accompanied the ritual, the spicy odors of the blazing sacrificial flame mingled with the pungent stench of the animal's innards. With a practiced grasp the sacrificers separated the glassy, bubbling intestines from the gaping body cavity of the bull, allowing them to slither into huge pitchers standing ready to one side.

Amunhotep III seemed fairly indifferent as he followed

40

the horrible event from his ebony-colored litter. Only when shanks and other great chunks of meat were distributed did he rise. Two servants came running to support the infirm pharaoh. As pieces of meat were handed to him one by one, Amunhotep threw them into the sacrificial flame.

This was the pharaoh's way of thanking the Lord of the Throne of the Two Lands, the god Amun, who had fulfilled his dearest wish after more than six years of waiting: to wed a young, light-skinned Mitanni princess, as beautiful as his "great royal wife," Tiy, had once been, when she was young. And now the time had come. Lookouts had reported that three barges were moving up the Nile, one of them holding the beautiful Princess Tadukhipa. By sundown the ships would be docking in Thebes.

Next, the general populace stepped out from behind the columns of the Temple of Karnak, and men and women dipped their fingers into the pools of blood to dot their foreheads with a crimson spot. This process was repeated several times, for slaves brought one bull after another, then antelopes, and finally geese. Temple dancers of both sexes, still almost children, accompanied by monotonous-sounding chorales, performed dances somewhat like rounds.

These dancers were taught in special schools affiliated with the temples. Most of them were no older than six when they commenced their training. There were only rumors of what happened to these children behind the walls of the temples—for whatever the priests did, they did for Amun, and what was done for Amun could not and should not be wrong.

The sun was already high above the holy Valley of the Kings when eight servants carried the black litter holding

The royal barge.

the pharaoh down to the Nile. The white, gold-trimmed royal barge Splendor of the Aten was about to dock at the red-reflecting marble steps leading to the shore. On a pedestal at the center of the ship stood a kind of large cage covered with thin white veils. Behind these one could recognize the outlines of the young Mitanni princess, who was staring excitedly at this new world.

Any stranger who, like Nefertiti, traveled up the Nile by boat and gazed for the first time on the bizarre and colorful metropolis of Thebes must have been nearly blinded by the glitter and gold. The country houses of the rich marched down to the shores of the Nile, each with flower-bedecked front gardens, dovetailed without system, overarched by the monumental sacred buildings, obelisks, and pylons which Homer erroneously called gates. (Thebes, "city of the hundred gates," had none, since it had never been walled in.)

And all the sights were enhanced by the clamor of traders from the world over, who congregated here because the residents of this city were more easily parted from their gold than people elsewhere. The ships thronged the harbor, and the commands of the overseers who were unloading stones from Aswan, fruit from Syria, wine casks from the Greek islands, and cattle from Lower Egypt rang out across the water.

The labyrinth of narrow streets always reeked of roasted meat and fish, and the stench of the open sewers pervaded the air. There was no proper canalization; only the elegant houses along the riverbank channeled their sewage into the Nile. Myriads of flies pursued every warm-blooded creature, sparing neither the pharaohs nor—as is shown by funerary paintings in the Valley of the Kings—the "great royal wives."

When the barge was moored at the shore, two women servants threw back the veiling over the cage. A petite young girl, only about fifteen years old, rose from her seat. Two fanbearers appeared behind her, holding huge plumed fans to keep the slanting rays of the sun from striking the face of the princess.

Pharaoh and people alike were struck by the young woman's extraordinary beauty. The princess from the north had a delicate face with large almond-shaped eyes; she was slender and graceful, and less than five feet tall. Most of all, however, the Egyptians were impressed by her pale coloring. Her skin color is a sure sign that Nefertiti was a princess rather than a woman of low origins. In those days aristocratic pallor was considered a crucial criterion for beauty, and only a king was able to shield his daughters from every ray of sunlight throughout their childhood.

With her eyes lowered, but showing unusual self-assurance for such a young woman, Tadukhipa climbed the marble steps from the shore to the terrace where Amunhotep III was waiting. He had left his litter and held out both hands in her direction. Tadukhipa walked toward the pharaoh, and while Amunhotep bowed to her, she raised her head very slightly. In doing so, their noses touched—that is, they kissed Egyptian fashion. Each said something that was incomprehensible to the other, both speaking their own tongues. The interpreters were not required to spring into action just yet, since the friendly nods of the two principals indicated that it was simply a matter of the usual compliments. Only when the pharaoh turned around and introduced the little princess to his "great royal wife," Tiy, did the scene take on a degree of cordiality. After a short greeting Amunhotep, Tadukhipa, and Tiy boarded the royal barge and made for the far shore of the Nile, followed by the two ships carrying Tadukhipa's companions and servants.

Surely Nefertiti was impressed by the opulence and splendor of this, the greatest and most handsome city in the world. But what must she have been feeling when she caught her first sight of this king, so old and sick and yet so lavishly furnished?

His spongy torso was bare, his obese hips girded with a long apron tied at the waist. Attached to his belt was a leopard's tail, dangling almost to the ground; like the blind uraeus—the emblematic cobra—whose effigy circled the pharaoh's forehead, this tail was a symbol of power. Amunhotep's "blue crown" made of leather was really nothing more than a kind of cap, but the pharaoh preferred it to the white cone-shaped crown of Upper Egypt, and even to the tall double crown of the united lands. Crooks, whips, cudgels, scepters, and swords were chosen to fit each occasion by officers of the wardrobe especially charged with this task.

Soon the great royal palace began to loom up on the opposite shore. When Nefertiti walked through the palace of Malkata for the first time, her feet stepped across shiny floors painted to look like a pond studded with lotus blossoms, with fish and ducks swimming through the water and transparent dragonflies and birds of brightly colored plumage darting among the reeds and flowering plants. An azure sky against which doves and large red butterflies fluttered was spread over the ceiling of the great hall. The walls glittered with gold, plant-shaped ornaments fashioned of glass stretched exuberantly to the roof, and all this glory was constantly permeated with the sweetish scent of incense and myrrh.

There were pieces of furniture and ornamental vases such as Nefertiti had never seen before. Chairs and footstools had legs so long and spindly that the princess from Mitanni was afraid to sit on them—for at home the only furniture was massive and heavy. Here one could see marvelous examples of wooden inlay work; the many boxes of ointments, scents, and odoriferous substances scattered throughout were not chiseled out of solid marble but were carved of translucent alabaster, hinting at their contents. Chests inlaid with scenes from the life of Amunhotep III and his "great royal wife," Tiy, bulged with jewelry and utensils made of gold.

Such, then, was the city over which "the magnificent" ruled. We must wonder whether Nefertiti was more deeply affected by her husband's ugliness or by the beauty of his metropolis.

For the beautiful princess, the day began early in the

morning, soon after sunrise. This custom was as com-
monplace as was the fact that bedtime took place soon after sundown. Nefertiti awoke to the scent of fresh myrrh
and the sounds of an all-girl band. A serving woman whose
job it was to check for the moment when Nefertiti would
open her eyes immediately drew the sail-like linen sheet
from the window of the huge sleeping chamber to let in the
first golden rays of the Aten.

Nefertiti slept alone. Her bed—by today's standards narrow and short—was made of precious ebony, trimmed with
artful inlays of wood, metal, and semiprecious stones. The
goat-hair mattress was covered with a fine white linen
cloth. Another sheet served to cover the queen; its purpose
must have been to ward off flies rather than to provide
warmth. Nefertiti slept in the nude.

A chamber next to the bedroom served as her dressing
room. Here a flock of serving women waited, each with a
specific task. One assisted the princess in choosing the garment for the day, one handed her the sandals she selected,
another the necklace, still another the headdress, and another the crown—unless Nefertiti preferred to remain
naked, which in those days was quite common among the
upper class. Only laborers and farmers who had to work
outdoors never went unclothed.

After arising came the bath. A daily bath was not considered in any way a luxury in ancient Egypt. The priests of
Amun practiced cleanliness to such an extent that in the
course of a day they managed to have four tub baths. But
even poor people bathed at least once a day. Either they
had their own bathroom, often furnished only with a
simple stone trough, or if they could not manage even this

much, they jumped into the Nile for a refreshing dip.

In the great palace of Thebes both the royal wife and every secondary wife—including Nefertiti, of course—had her own bathroom. The tub, raised on a marble pedestal, was made of translucent alabaster. Several dozen serving women brought water in gold and silver jugs. At a gesture from the young queen, two more servants poured fragrant essences from smaller pitchers into the bath water until another gesture from their mistress bade them stop. Ancient Egyptians loved strong scents. All who cared anything about themselves and who could afford it creamed, oiled, and dabbed their bodies with precious essences.

Next it was time for Nefertiti to dress. She usually wore a voluminous, diaphanous white garment that emphasized rather than concealed her gentle curves. The deep, low neckline was framed by a broad collar of gold and semiprecious stones fashioned to imitate a wreath of petals of the blue lotus and fruits of the persea tree.

Nefertiti's non-Egyptian looks were emphasized by the fact that she liked to hide her long hair under a blue headdress such as was normally worn only by Asiatic queens. (Since blue was the color of the gods—and thus of rulers as well—the headdress gives an additional clue to her royal birth.) This characteristic hat was lined in golden yellow; it was six and a half inches high, and an inch-wide ribbon was wound around its center, studded with carnelians and malachite between narrow gold bands and lapis lazuli inserts. The ribbon ended at the back of the head in three tails ornamented by a carnelian stud with two papyrus clusters to either side.

Thus attired, Nefertiti was finally ready to appear in

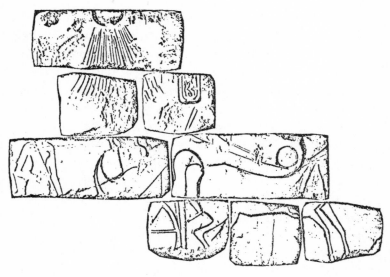

Nefertiti goes driving in her own chariot. (This picture was reconstructed by computer.)

public. On her walks through the metropolis, which she undertook with an entourage of serving women, she must have visited the homes of many wealthy Thebans. These homes were really miniature palaces.

The ground floor of a Theban residence was generally approached across flat steps through a double-winged door. The visitor then stood in a whitewashed hall whose walls were bordered above and below by a flower-and-garland frieze. Four brightly painted wooden pillars supported the blue-colored ceiling. The windows, which often extended down to the floor, were—if facing south—walled with open brickwork, so that there was a view of the outside and a light breeze could waft through the house. These pierced walls were a novelty, for most of the houses of the period received light only through the door openings or an opening at the lintel.

Ceramic tiles or raw bricks formed the floor, which was covered with rush matting or brightly colored rugs. On these stood the furniture—dainty chairs of ebony with inlays of ivory, chests and cupboards covered with crushed gold and decorated with precious stones, couches woven of palm leaves and upholstered with pillows of leather and cloth. A stone pedestal in every room offered space for a movable heater which, filled with glowing charcoal, could be carried from room to room on a cold day.

In a Theban home there were many rooms, some houses being built as high as three stories. The wives—of whom a Theban tended to have several—were particularly fond of congregating on the flat roof. The principal wife was assigned her own apartments in her husband's house, complete with separate chambers for her serving women. The husband's manservants also had their own rooms, usually in an outbuilding apart from the main house.

There was more than one of every kind of room—several dining rooms (each with its own washing facility) and a number of bedrooms (each flanked by a washroom and a toilet). Cooking was done in a separate building, which also contained the storerooms. A mansion naturally required a garden. The pond designed for bathing was also stocked with waterfowl, and water plants floated on it.

Great banquets were held in these magnificent homes, and Nefertiti must have attended many of them. In the living lounge she would have seen an illustrious crowd of lightly clad guests, the ladies in simple, long garments—cut very low, many of them exposing their shoulders or concealing only one breast—and the men in brief loincloths.

A serving man carrying jugs of water and bowls went from guest to guest to wash their hands while a second servant followed to dry them. Still another wrapped the company in clouds of incense, and a fourth placed a scented cone of fat on the head of each. These cones were enriched with all sorts of aromatic essences that were released only when the fat began to melt as a result of increasing body temperature. This custom was considered elegant and the height of luxury. Rivulets running from the scented cones across hair, face, and clothing were never wiped away.

Both the men and the women who made up the distinguished company wore wigs; only the servants appeared in the glory of their natural curls. Highly scented lotus blossoms were intertwined in the ladies' huge hairdos, while the men held lotus blossoms between their fingers, ready to hand them to the belle of their choice.

Eating was not done at a long table; rather, guests were furnished with individual trays on legs set with whole ducks, lamb shanks, and a plethora of fruit. Wine and a kind of beer, drunk from silver and gold cups, were poured from tall pitchers that narrowed toward the bottom so that they required holders to stay upright. There was no silverware, only fingers.

The servants were always prepared for vomiting guests; they would stand behind them, ready with funnel-shaped containers for the eventuality. Musicians performed on dainty flutes, crashing cymbals, and harps that stood as tall as a man and gave off sonorous sounds. Between the various instrumental selections, singers performed songs proclaiming the joy of life as well as some whose lyrics expressed contemporary criticism. At an advanced hour, when the oil lamps fed with salted castor oil threw shadows on the walls, a special attraction was offered: beautiful dancers swaying to the beat of the music, dressed in nothing but a golden chain around their slender waists or a colorful garland circling their throats.

Unlike the custom of the Romans in a later age, attendance at banquets in Thebes was by no means restricted to men, as many depictions in tombs of the New Kingdom make clear. The extent to which women were able to hold their liquor at times can be deduced from one such tomb relief, which shows a drinking woman who says, "Give me eighteen cups of wine. See, I wish to drink to the point of drunkenness. My insides are as dry as straw."

Alcoholism and prostitution flourished, especially among the young people. "I am told that you have left your work and are chasing pleasures," a teacher admonished his student. "You go from street to street, as long as there is the smell of beer, until you perish. Beer chases men away from you. It brings ruin to your soul. You are like a broken wheel on a ship, unable to respond in any direction. You are like a temple without a god, like a house without bread. You loiter about with the loose girls and have taken on their smell. Your wreath of flowers hangs around your neck, and you drum on your belly. You stumble, and then you fall on your face and are spotted with mud."

And a worried father, the wise Ani, warned his son against drunkenness. "Do not boast of being able to drink a whole pitcher of beer. You speak, and an incomprehensible stutter comes from your mouth. If you fall and break your limbs, no one will extend a hand to you. Your drinking companions stand up and say, 'Away with this fool!' If someone comes to ask you a question, he finds you lying on the floor, as helpless as a little child.''

The first Theban religious festival in which Nefertiti participated may have reminded her of the oriental pomp at home in Mitanni—though the extravagance practiced in golden Thebes must have overshadowed anything the princess had known before. Each year, on New Year's Day, the great feast in honor of Amun was celebrated. To honor the god, the pharaoh and his retinue paraded from the temple at Karnak to the "southern harem," the temple in Luxor. The scene is preserved for us in a depiction on the walls of the temple's great hall of pillars, though the paintings themselves date from the slightly later era of Tutankhamun. His successor, Horemheb, made some additional changes, but the festival does not differ a great deal as far as pageantry and splendor are concerned from the Amun festival as Amunhotep III and Nefertiti celebrated it.

Clouds of incense pervaded the Holy of Holies of the great temple of Karnak, where, among the celestial sounds of scantily clad, rhythmically swaying female temple musicians, the pharaoh brought offerings of food and drink to the god Amun, his wife, Mut, and their son, Khonsu. The sweet scent of the incense mixed penetratingly with the stench of seething fat dripping from beef shanks and carefully eviscerated rams into the blazing sacrificial fire.

Because the pharaoh was eager to display his new wife to the people, Nefertiti was made to join the aging Tiy in following the second barge in the great procession now forming in the temple. The procession was led by a trumpeter, who flung his flourishes into the blue-flickering morning sky, closely attended by drum rolls. Behind the musicians marched the censer, carrying a large golden container of smoldering scented incense. He in turn was followed by the high priest, shaved bald, and naked except for a loincloth of leopard skin. Then came the barge of the sun god as well as two more boats.

The three barges of Amun, Mut, and Khonsu stood all year at a special location in the temple, which was called "the great site." They rested on a trapeze-shaped pedestal artfully carved of stone. At the place that was normally reserved for the helmsman a shrine concealed a wooden idol about three feet high. Diaphanous veils were draped over the shrine. The barges were ordinary, seaworthy ships, though ornately wrought. The ceremonies—a part of the sun cult of Heliopolis—were based on the concept that the sun god commands a ship that sails across the shining sky by day and is rowed through the underworld at night.

The sides of the barges were pierced by horizontal poles, so that each could be carried by twenty-four Amun priests. It was an impressive sight to watch these ascetic figures marching at a carefully rehearsed pace down to the life-giving Nile carrying the veiled barges on their shoulders, framed by two bearers with huge, costly plumed fans at the bow and stern of each barge and two accompanying priests at port and starboard. (The Amun priests considered themselves seamen. In every temple the order of the priesthood was divided into four watches or phyla. As on the high seas, these watches—named after the four parts of a ship—were called the bow watch, the stern watch, the port watch, and the starboard watch.)

Amunhotep III marched behind the barge of the sun god,

while Nefertiti and the "great royal wife" followed the barge of the goddess Mut. The populace was surely less interested in the magnificent ceremonies than in the young, beautiful Mitanni princess, light-skinned and rosy, walking at the side of Tiy, just turned fifty and burned brown by the eternal sun of Egypt. They must have made an unlikely pair.

Arrived at the shores of the Nile, the priests pulled the sacred barges across the pillar-flanked marble steps, past the blazing bowls of burning oil, and set them down on the great ships of the royal fleet. These ships in turn were hauled upstream by long ropes pulled by slaves until they reached Luxor, while the three sacred barges on board the great Nile boats glittered in the sun.

Amunhotep III was proud of his ships; they had been crafted by the best artisans in the land. The largest was composed of "new cedarwood which His Majesty had felled in the mountains of Tonuter [Lebanon] and which had been brought across the mountains of Retenu by the lords of all foreign lands. It is very broad and long. Never before has anything of the kind been constructed. It is over-laid with silver and inlaid all over with gold. The great shrine is of gold, and it fills the land with its glow." The poop of the ship bore the crowns of Upper and Lower Egypt emblazoned with the cobra; silken banners fluttered from golden masts. Two priestesses playing instruments—the Mert priestesses—danced around the Holy of Holies, uttering cries of jubilation that were answered by the Thebans marching upstream on the eastern shore, keeping pace with the ships.

On land an Amun priest headed the procession, singing a hymn in honor of the sun god.

Hail to thee, Amun-Re, most beautiful of each day
Who rises unendingly in the morning,
Khepre, who struggles with the works,
Your rays are in the countenance
Without our knowing.
Gold is not to be compared with your splendor.
You are Ptah, you shape your limbs,
You are creator without being created,
You are the unique one who hastens through eternity,
Who leads millions of men on the paths.
Your splendor is like the splendor of heaven,
Your color glows more brightly than its cloak.
When you pass along the sky,
The world regards you,
Though your path is hidden from them.
When you show yourself in the morning,
The day's work increases.
When you drive along in majesty,
The day is nothing.
When you hasten along the way,
Millions and hundreds of thousands of men are only a
    moment.
Each day is subject to you
By hurrying toward your setting,
And you complete the hours of the night in the same
    manner.
You have divided them
Without a cessation in your work being noticed.
All eyes see through you,
They can do nothing when your majesty sets.
You arise very early to rise in the morning.
Your rays open eyes,
When you set in the western mountain,
They sleep like the dead.

Behind the singing Amun priests an escort of soldiers

bearing spears and shields marched to muffled drum rolls. They formed a strong contrast to the jugglers and dancing Africans, to the singing and dancing priestesses and priests who followed, shaking castanets and sistras (ancient Egyptian rattling musical instruments that were spread with the cult of Isis). Finally, a furthur delegation of Amun priests and lute players were followed by the Theban people, in high spirits as at every festival, beating the rhythm of the music with their hands.

At the mooring place in Luxor the pageantry that had taken place at the departure in Karnak was repeated. The barges were taken from the ships and carried to the temple before the pharaoh and his consorts. Amunhotep III had had the temple built for Amun, Mut, and Khonsu at the site of an older shrine. Measuring 190 by 55 yards, it was not as large as the temple of Karnak, but it was no less splendid. While the Thebans continued to shout with joy, the priests hauled the barge through the great pylon at the northern entrance and along Amunhotep's fifty-five-yard-long hall of pillars. The second court was encircled by a double row of columns, and at its rear wall a forecourt with thirty-two papyrus-bundle pillars opened out.

Amunhotep sacrificed to the gods cf Luxor. The barges were set down in the Holy of Holies while the king entered the twelve-pillared hall where the table for offerings stood. Delegations from each province of Upper and Lower Egypt stepped forward to present their sacrificial gifts.

The "southern harem," the temple of Luxor, was dedicated to Amun, for the pharaoh was taken to be the bodily son of Amun, the god of Thebes. Accordingly, the wife of the pharaoh was the wife of the god, and the "southern ha-

Head of a colossal statue of Hatshepsut, about 4 feet high with beard, of painted limestone. (From one of the Osiris colossi of the queen at Deir el Bahri.)

rem of Amun" was his "palace." Until the time of Amunhotep III the wife of the god—that is, the queen—was also the first among the "harem women of Amun," the priestesses. A room next to the Holy of Holies in the Luxor temple and the Hatshepsut temple of Deir el Bahri contain pictures of the conception and birth of the pharaoh; many Egyptologists, such as the English scholar Aylward Blackman, see this as a reference to a kind of cultic sexual intercourse. The union of the divine pharaoh and the wife of the god, in the opinion of these scholars, took place while the populace sang and danced outside the gates of the innermost temple.

It may be assumed that this attempt to conceive a god— if it was still undertaken at all by Amunhotep III, who was already seriously ill—must have been quite a shock to the fifteen-year-old Nefertiti, and it can only have had a negative influence on her attitude toward the Egyptian worship of Amun.

What went on at this ritual intercourse is reported by the priestly scribes of the New Kingdom.

> This splendid god Amun, the lord of the "throne of both lands," having assumed the form of his majesty her husband, the king of Upper and Lower Egypt, came to her. He found her as she lay sleeping in the beauty of her palace. She was awakened by the god's odor and she laughed in the presence of his majesty. He came directly to her, burned for her, and gave her his heart. He let her see him in his divine shape as he came before her. She was glad when she saw his beauty, and love for him coursed through her body. The palace was flooded with the scent of the god; all his odors were like those of Punt. Then the majesty of the god did with her all he desired. She let him pleasure himself in her.

But the gods were not the only ones to have reason for rejoicing. The people, too, were not made to suffer want. The temples were all provided with storage chambers, and on days such as this their doors were opened and the food and drink they held were available to anyone. Genuine orgies of wantonness were played out. All day long there was dancing, eating, and drinking, as is vividly represented in a Theban inscription.

> The gods of heaven sing with joy, the Hathors [music-making priestesses representing the goddess Hathor] clash their cymbals, the inhabitants are drunk with wine, wreaths of flowers cover their heads. The rowing crew [of the royal fleet] wanders about joyfully, anointed with the most precious oil. All the children are enjoying themselves—from the rise of the sun to its setting.

If ever there was a time when the art of celebrating was invented, it was here, in wealthy Thebes. Ships from Palestine and Syria, from Cyprus and other countries sailed up the Nile through the delta, and caravans arrived from every direction, from the land of Punt and from Asia, to deliver every luxury article known to this world in Thebes, either as tribute or in exchange for jingling coin. Money—here it really was of no account.

At that time the question of how many wives a sophisticated man indulged in was purely a financial one. In ancient Thebes a new wife contributed a great deal to a man's standing—the larger the harem, the greater the prestige he enjoyed. Like all Egyptians, Thebans lived in monogamy—that is, "the wife of the house" was the only legal wife, the mother of the heir. But if a man wished to possess several wives, there was no need for him to thwart his desires. He enrolled them as secondary wives in his harem. These secondary wives only rarely competed with the "wife of the house"; they were concubines, nothing more. Their sole task consisted of sweetening their master's nights; in exchange they enjoyed free room and board.

Concubines generally came from the lower social classes. Attractive girls exploited the glow of youth to rise on the social scale through marriage with an aristocratic or rich man. Nor is it any secret that now and again a concubine did make the attempt to contend with the lady of the house for her position.

There is only one explanation for the fact that Tiy did not regard the young Nefertiti as a rival and did not simply dispatch her behind the walls of the harem, like so many other of Amunhotep's wives. (Of the many women

Amunhotep III married in his lifetime, we know the names of only five.) The singular cause of Tiy's cordiality lies in what may have been the common origin of both women—Mitanni. They may have enjoyed the same upbringing, they may have been related to each other through shared memories of their homeland. And even if in his old age Amunhotep III shared his bed with the young Nefertiti—though this is by no means proven, various facts even arguing against it—officially Tiy remained his "only beloved great royal wife." And the lack of tension may well have been the result of an agreement between the two women not to get in each other's way.

Tiy totally dominated her old, sick husband. Indeed, we have no evidence of the pharaoh's initiating any political action after the tenth year of his reign, when the sensual king was still at the height of his powers. Amunhotep III showed no interest in sports, much less in warfare. He was by no means a pacifist; he was simply lazy. He watched indifferently as the Nile flooded the fields and fertilized the land year after year; idly he followed the uprisings of the vassals. Amunhotep III fed on the power and wealth of his ancestors.

It can be taken for certain that at least from the year 1366 B.C. on, when the king's state of health deteriorated to such an extent that he required King Tushratta to send the statue of Ishtar, which promised relief, Tiy held absolute power in her hands. This state of affairs is supported by the letter Tushratta sent to her immediately upon the death of Amunhotep III, as well as by Tiy's own letters abroad. Only one other "great royal wife" ever carried on a separate correspondence with other potentates. That was—twenty years later—Nefertiti.

Nefertiti, already self-assured and of high intelligence in spite of her fifteen years, was forced to accept Tiy's proposition, whether she wanted to or not. But we can easily imagine that she watched each of the old queen's steps carefully.

Son of my flesh, my darling Nebmaatre, my living image who has gone forth from me. . . . My heart rejoices mightily when it beholds your beauty. I perform wonders for your majesty so that you will grow young again.

—*Words of the god Amun on a stela of Amunhotep III at Thebes*

4 | DEATH OF A PHARAOH

The year is 1364 B.C. The wonder-working statue of Ishtar, which Tushratta had sent along with his daughter, had been intended to help the critically ill pharaoh. The populace was curious to find out whether the mysterious Asiatic goddess installed in the palace of Malkata would prove to be stronger than the gods of Egypt.

Then the distressing news spread. "The Majesty of Horus, Strong Bull, Appeared in Truth, Golden Horus, Great in Strength, Who Defeats the Asiatics, the King of Upper and Lower Egypt, Nebmaatre, the son of Re Amunhotep, ruler of Thebes, is dead."

Criers carried the tidings to all parts of the city, couriers sped off to the farthest provinces of the realm to broadcast the message: Egypt was without a pharaoh.

How old was the king at the time of his death? No fewer than sixteen inscriptions have been found that mention the thirty-eighth year of Amunhotep III's reign, but no surviving record mentions a thirty-ninth year. Therefore it is fairly certain that the pharaoh died in the thirty-eighth year of his reign—that is, at the age of about fifty to fifty-five. When she was seventeen years old, Nefertiti was already a widow.

By tradition, the oldest son and successor of the deceased pharaoh was obligated to take care of the interment. But since Amunhotep IV was either out of the country or simply too young, the great royal wife Tiy had to see to the burial. Though Nefertiti, as a secondary wife of the pharaoh, had no official function in this ritual, there can be little doubt that she took part in the ceremonies. While the death of the sick old man may, on the one hand, have seemed like a deliverance to her, on the other, the seventeen-year-old girl could look to an uncertain future, dependent as she was on Tiy's favor.

Though her grief may not have been too deeply felt, Nefertiti did go into mourning. Her dress was a loose white sack that hung down in numerous pleats. As a further sign of grief, she put a halt to her daily bathing and, like all the women of the harem, scattered dirt on her head.

From earliest times the Egyptians wondered what happened to the godlike pharaoh after his demise, and throughout the years they developed some astonishing beliefs. Originally they assumed the dead pharaoh to be among the stars in the sky or among the birds in the trees, the cranes in the water and the beetles in the sand. Finally, however, they arrived at the understanding that the dead pharaoh was to be looked for "on the beautiful paths" in the underworld through which the sun god Re drove nightly.

Particular difficulties presented themselves to the Egyptians in their concepts of the hereafter through the "split personality" of man. They believed that the human being was composed of body, soul (ba), and guardian spirit (ka). The ka was the crucial element; longevity, good and bad fortune, illness and good health, strength or weakness—the ka was responsible for all of them. Identical double images were generally made to represent the dead pharaoh with his ka, "the living ka of the lord of both lands, the victorious bull who shines in Thebes." According to the Egyptian conception, the ka did not die; rather, at some time it returned to the lifeless shell of the body. And that was why the corpse had to be preserved; that was why realistic statuettes of the deceased were part of the funerary furnishings. The table with offerings of food and drink in the pharaoh's tomb was intended for the nourishment of the ka, not for the mummy. And Tiy and Nefertiti may have joined in murmuring the traditional formula for the enjoyment of the funerary fare of the third Amunhotep:

> An offering which the king gives
> An offering which Anubis gives,
> Thousands of bread, beer,
> Oxen, geese,
> For the ka of the great Nebmaatre.

On the evening of the day of the pharaoh's death, when the sun had already set, the ghastly ritual of his mummification—a three-month process—began by torchlight.

In a cool, windowless outbuilding of the Malkata palace a surgical team of funerary priests prepared the corpse of Amunhotep III. Each priest was ready to perform his special task. The first, using red ink, marked the line of a vertical incision on the left side of the abdomen. The dissector instantly drew his knife and with a few sawing motions opened the dead pharaoh's abdominal wall. No sooner had the incision been made than the priest dropped his knife, gathered up his long garment, and ran from the dissecting room. The other mummifiers threw stones after him— stones that were already at hand. This was the way it had to be done according to the age-old rite, for men who inflicted bodily damage on others were considered evil, persons who must be punished.

After this short ceremony another dissector stepped forward. With a practiced gesture he reached into the gaping abdominal cavity and pulled out the entrails one after another: heart, liver, kidneys, lungs, intestines; after repeated washings, they were individually placed in four stone jugs standing ready for the purpose. These visceral jars, also called canopic vases, were shut with stone lids to capture the inner organs, the supposed bearers of the senses—hunger and thirst in particular. Each vessel was dedicated to one of the sons of the god Horus.

In order to reach the brain, the nasal septum was carved open with a special chisel. Using a silver hook, which he thrust diagonally upward through the nasal passage, the third dissector finally pulled the brain out of the cranium. Then the corpse was ready for the process of desiccation, which took seventy days and was achieved through seasoning the corpse in natron. This treatment is only one of the secrets of why mummies barely change their appearance in three or four thousand years.

While the desiccation was occurring, feverish activity went on in the western declivity of the Valley of the Kings to complete the rock tomb of Amunhotep III. During his lifetime the king had begun the excavations, but like so many pharaohs, he took up the venture too late, so that during the final ninety days the work had to go on at a furious pace. Sculptors chopped the final niches into the rock, painters laid on the last coats of color and sketched in the final texts, while the masters of the ordnance began to put together the equipment for eternity. The construction of royal tombs was carried out in complete secrecy. Only a few were initiated into the details of the project. Ineni, the architect of the tomb of Thutmose I, says in a document which was found in his own tomb, "I inspected the excavation of the cliff-tomb of His Majesty—alone, no one seeing, no one hearing."

The artists and artisans who for some five hundred years created the tombs of the immortal pharaohs were called "servants at the abode of truth." They lived in their own village of about fifty houses, surrounded by a wall, near the approach to the rocky Valley of the Kings. The labor in this camp of gravediggers was strictly organized under the "leader of the work." He was aided by architects, foremen, and scribes. Painters and sculptors formed a separate guild, as did quarrymen and bricklayers; unskilled laborers and muleteers had the least prestige. Twice a month a small caravan of heavily laden donkeys arrived to provide the workers with drinking water, provisions, and working materials. Dried meat and fish, flat bread, and legumes were the general fare, as were onions for the prevention of infectious diseases.

The "servants at the abode of truth" were better paid than other workers, their annual wages corresponding to

On reverse: The unforgettable bust of Queen Nefertiti, 12 inches tall, from the workshop of Thutmose the sculptor. Painted limestone with stucco surfacing. (Egyptian Museum, Berlin.)

Above: This head of black basalt, 24 inches high, of a gigantic statue from the earliest regnal years of Amunhotep III, portrays the pharaoh as a young man. (Brooklyn Museum, New York.)

Below: An uncompleted head, 13 inches tall, of Queen Nefertiti in rose quartzite. (National Museum, Cairo.)

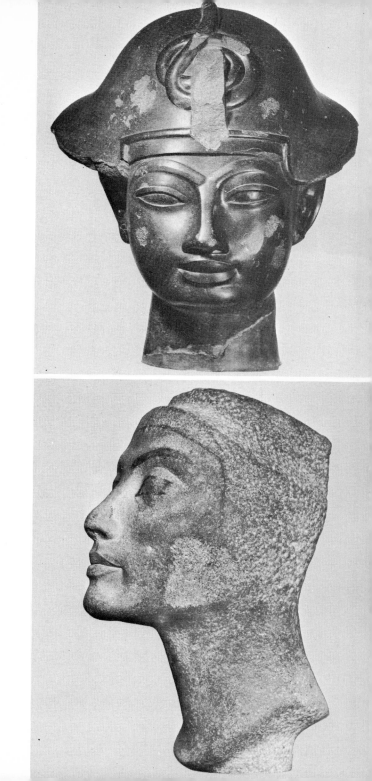

Portrait of Queen Tiy in old age, carved from yew, 27 inches high. (Egyptian Museum, Berlin.)

Partial view of one of the monumental figures depicting the pharaoh Akhenaten from the temple of the Aten in Karnak. (National Museum, Cairo.)

the price of a bull. Many were paid in food and clothing. It was quite common to pay even the higher officials and military personnel in kind—with plots of land or with prisoners of war who were then employed as domestic servants.

Two Egyptologists, Georg Steindorff and Walther Wolf, suppose that captives were used to work on the tombs, and that after completing their labors they were put to death. That, however, is pure speculation for which no documentation can be found. What good would it have done, anyway, to kill the workmen on the tomb and rock—after all, sculptors, painters, plasterers, scribes, masters of the ordnance, and priests also knew about the site. And it is certain that they were not killed.

Since Amunhotep III was such a significant pharaoh, the masters of the ordnance furnished his tomb with beds of state and beds for resting, chests and shrines, armchairs and footstools, dishes and ornamental vases, even luxurious chariots and ships. Hundreds of ushabti figures—tiny carvings of people—were designed to perform every kind of work for the dead king in the hereafter. For the Elysian fields, ruled over by the god of death, Osiris, were not only paradise, such as we, shaped by Christian doctrine, imagine them to be. There was work to be done as on earth, especially work in the fields. These labors were to be performed for the pharaoh by the little figurines, on which the appropriate activity was often indicated. And so that they would be able to manage their chores, they were given miniature tools—hoes for tilling the soil, flails for threshing, baskets for harvesting.

The ancient Egyptian concept that a naturalistic representation of a person could bring that person to life in the

Egyptian gods and goddesses from tombs from the period of the New King-dom. From left to right, top: Ptah, Hathor, Thot, Osiris; bottom: Isis, An-ubis, Amun.

hereafter went so far that the pharaohs, who during their lifetime held sway over a large harem, were given statuettes of naked women in their tombs, and these were intended to help their lord pass the time in the beyond. These doll-like figurines were made of stone, wood, or faience—and they became coveted souvenirs of the earliest excavators in the nineteenth century.

Since in spite of all possible forethought, the future in the kingdom of the dead still remained highly uncertain, the Egyptians did not stint on amulets and talismans as gifts in the tomb. There were Horus eyes, papyrus pillars, finger amulets, and wonder-working scarabs—and all had but one purpose: to confer magical powers on the mummy when they were hung around its neck or tied to its chest.

No people in the history of humanity have put such a great value on the equipment of a tomb appropriate to the personality of the deceased as have the Egyptians. After the interment the tombs were walled up for all eternity, so the care applied by the builders to the interior walls can only be explained as a sign of their profound belief in the continuation of life after death.

The tomb Amunhotep III had built for himself represents the end of the development of the Egyptian art of tomb building as far as technical construction is concerned. Chambers and corridors are at right angles to each other. We do not, therefore, find an unsystematic labyrinth, as in the tomb of Thutmose III, in which every corridor and every chamber is at a different angle from the preceding one, and only one of the eight chambers is rectangular.

The tomb of Amunhotep III was entered by a long, steep staircase. From it, a corridor led farther downward to a second staircase, and at its lower end a diagonal walk continued in the same direction. It ended in a square pit which gave access to a rectangular anteroom to the left; at the center of this, two pillars supported the ceiling. From here a right-angle staircase led downward, giving access to a further diagonal walk and another stairway. This ended in still another rectangular antechamber. Along the left wall a short corridor led to a hall with four pillars, behind which lay the crypt with a hall of one pillar. Along the two long walls of the four-pillar hall and the adjacent crypt lay two subsidiary chambers, each for utensils.

From the art historian's point of view, the tomb of Amunhotep III is very special. Since the eleventh dynasty the funerary texts were inscribed in color on the white-washed walls. In their book *Die thebanische Gräberwelt*, Steindorff and Wolf write:

> This custom, which continued into the first half of the eighteenth dynasty for private tombs, was adopted for the royal tombs. And not only the texts were painted on the walls in hieratic script; pictures pertaining to them—which after all are the main thing and are clarified by the text— are also presented in evocative sketches. Not until the tomb of Amunhotep III was a pictorial style approached in the pictures, and starting with Horemheb, both text and pictures were cast in complete pictorial form and equated to the contemporary relief style which attained its indisputable climax subsequently in the tomb of Seti.

Although Amunhotep III had begun to build his tomb early—though not early enough—it remained uncompleted, and only one of the four halls as well as parts of the corridors were provided with pictures and texts. But the pharaoh had to be buried, the tomb had to be sealed; and so we will probably never learn more than we know today about the death of Amunhotep III or about Nefertiti's relationship with him.

After dehydration in natron for about seventy days, the

corpse of Amunhotep III was washed and treated with palm wine, incense, cedar oil, myrrh, and cinnamon; these ointments and perfumes had a preservative effect. Finally the mummifiers went into action. They wrapped the torso and limbs in linen bandages. Between the individual layers of cloth they painted on a kind of gummy solution, the ingredients of which are unknown to us. It has been shown that the Egyptians spent thousands of years experimenting with the constituents of the solution. Thus there were solutions that preserved the mummies well and others that actually burned the bandages and body tissues, so that many mummies look black today—surely not the mummifiers' intention.

The Greek historian Herodotus, who dealt exhaustively with the history of ancient Egypt in the fifth century b.c., also gave a fairly detailed description of the mummification technique. Dr. Zaki Iskander, former general director of the Department of Antiquities in Cairo, who made extensive studies of mummification practices, came to the conclusion that on the whole Herodotus's descriptions were accurate. As Iskander, notes, the corpses—including even the obese Amunhotep III—were stuffed with herbs, straw, and wads of cloth during the dehydration process, so that no malformations would set in. The resin or mastic clumps with which the nostrils, cheeks, and arm and leg muscles of Amunhotep III were stuffed, however, hardened to such an extent that— as described in chapter 3—they even screened the X rays taken by Harris and Weeks three thousand years later.

Through a lucky circumstance the ritual of embalming has been handed down to us in almost every detail. Two independent papyri, dating from different periods, contain the instructions and incantations for mummification. One, the Cairo papyrus, presumably comes from Thebes and was intended for "the priest of Amun-Re and Bastet in Thebes, Heter, son of Harsiesis and Taiheru." The other, Louvre Papyrus 5158, was written "for the prophet of Amun-Re and the Bastet in Thebes, Horus, son of the dancing girl of Amun-Re and the priest of the rights of So-kar Isis."

The following quotation is taken from the more detailed and better-preserved Cairo papyrus. The first twenty-three lines are missing. The ritual begins with the anointing of the head.

> Then anoint his head twice with good oil of myrrh. A death priest speaks: "O Osiris, the oil of myrrh to you, which comes from Punt, to beautify your scent with the scent of the god. The effluvium to you who comes from Re; to beautify your body through the oil. Your soul rises on your body in the land of god."
>
> Next one should take an ointment vessel in which are kept the ten oils of the mouth opening. Apply it from his head and his elbow down to the soles of his feet, but take care not to anoint his head. [The ritual of the mouth opening was intended to restore to the deceased the use of his organs by an act of magic.]
>
> To this the death priest intones, "O Osiris, receive the 'Festival Scent' that beautifies your limbs. Receive the perfume so that you will unite with the great sun-god; it unites with you and strengthens your limbs; and you unite with Osiris in the great hall."
>
> Next put the entrails in a faience vessel from which the Horus children are anointed, and let the ointment of this god [the mummy] penetrate the divine limbs until the entrails are truly saturated with the fat.
>
> Next turn this god onto his stomach. Bathe his spine in the holy oil just mentioned, and leave the spine lying as it was on

earth until all the work of the "Beautiful House" [the work-
room of the embalmer] is done on him. Then lay a rolled-up
bandage on the bier. Turn his face toward heaven while his
spine lies in the oil on the garment of Sobk of Shedet [a city in
the Upper Egyptian province of Fayyum]....

Then lay his back with the ointment on the garment like
his shape was on earth. But take care that he does not fall
onto his coffin while his head and stomach are filled with
drugs, because the gods who are in his coffin would be
moved from their place. Next turn his face toward heaven,
as it was before.

Then gild the nails on his hands and his feet, beginning
with his fingers to his toes, which are wound around with a
bandage of linen from the weavers of Sais.... Now Anubis
[a priest who is costumed like the god Anubis, protector of
the necropolises] sits down below the head of this god, and
no kherheb [lector priest] may come near him, until the one
lying on the mystery has introduced every material into
him, except the guardian of the god, who reaches into the
head, the assistant of the one lying on the mystery. Then
anoint his head and his whole mouth with oil, and the back
of the head as well as the face.

Wind him in the bandage of Re-Herakhte from the city
of Hebt and the bandage of Nekhebt from el Kab, which is
laid against his forehead; and the bandage of Hathor, the
mistress of Dendera, which is laid against his face; and the
bandage of Thoth, who judged the two fighters, which is
laid against his ears; and the bandage of Nebthotpet, which
is laid against his forehead.

Each weave and each material on his head shall be made
of these bandages. The condition of these and the pictures
on them shall be examined by the one who is lying on the
mystery, for it is useful to appraise the finished drawings.

The bandage of Sakhmet, the powerful one, beloved of
Ptah, shall be made of two strips against his head. At his
two ears: two strips named "Mistress of Completion." At

the two nostrils: two strips, of which one is called Nehi, the other Smen. At the two cheeks: two strips named Hahtitisu. At the forehead: four strips named "the Flashing Ones." On top of the head: two strips named "Fillers of Both Uzat Eyes." Twenty-one strips are wound to the right and left of his face, around his ears. At his mouth: four strips, two inside, two outside. At the chin: two bandages named [illegible]. At the neck: four large strips.

Then the bandages should be rolled through a large strip of two fingers' breadth. While the openings in his head are stuffed, anoint him again with the thick oil previously mentioned. . . . Then repeatedly anoint the head with myrrh. . . . Anoint him again with oil, the head as well as the face. Lay seeds and fruits under his head. . . .

Next embalm this god. Dip his left hand, together with the fist, in the oil, previously mentioned, to which has been added: 1 part ankhyemi plant, 1 part resin from Koptos, 1 part natron. Then wrap his ears with a bandage of woven royal linen. His fingers and the nails on his hand should be properly straightened and wrapped. Then let a ring which has been prepared in the workshop be put around his male pride.

Place a golden ring on his finger and repeatedly lay gold into his fist. Then fill out his hand with stuff. First anoint his fingers on the outer side with the addition of ankhyemi plants, natron, and resin and divine material.

All this is to be done in thirty-six steps, because there are thirty-six gods with whom his soul ascends to heaven and thirty-six provinces where the shapes of Osiris reveal themselves.

Up to this point all the rituals were carried out by priests and skilled embalmers. In the treatment of the hands and legs that now followed, the sons of the deceased—who until then had stood attentively to the right and the left of the bier—became involved. The Cairo papyrus is very explicit

about this. The procedure was the same as already described. When at last the mummy was completely
wrapped, it was swathed once more in a cloud of incense
while the priests intoned one great final prayer.

After a mummification process that had taken nearly
three months, the time had finally come: Amunhotep III
was taken to his ultimate resting place. Unlike every other
burial of a pharaoh witnessed by the capital city of Thebes
up to that time, no great mourning procession formed
down to the Nile, where the mummy was taken across the
river to the Valley of the Kings. The new palace of
Amunhotep III already occupied the western shore of the
river, and in any case the people were not allowed to take
part in the ceremonies in the Valley of the Kings.

The mourning procession was preceded by a half-naked
priest, clad only in a leopard skin, who waved a censer and
intoned prayers: "A smoke offering to you who is in the
barge of the divine father Nun, in that Nekhmet barge that
carries the god and Isis and Nephthys and this Horus, the
son of Osiris."

Tiy walked behind the high priest. Her breasts were uncovered as a sign of grief. Nefertiti walked immediately behind her, followed by a group of the pharaoh's secondary
wives. Eight death priests, carrying the mummy case of the
king on their shoulders, marched behind them. Last came
the relatives, the court, and the officials with the gifts and
offerings they intended to place in the tomb of their deceased lord. Dancing girls and singing girls made up the
tail end of the procession.

The women wailed and lamented loudly when the procession arrived at the rock tomb of Amunhotep III. But the

open stone sarcophagus intended for the pharaoh was already occupied by the death, or sem, priest. Wrapped completely in bandages like a mummy, the sem priest had first to be awakened by the shouts of three men in a complicated ceremonial. Then he carried out the symbolic opening of the mouth. And it was not until this moment that the king's ka could escape through his mouth.

One last time Tiy symbolically embraced the mummy of her husband, with whom she had lived for almost four decades, and declaimed the funerary lament: "I am your sister—great one, do not leave me. You are so fair, my good father. That I am far from you now—how can that be? Now I walk alone. You, who used to like speaking with me, you are silent now and speak no more."

While servants and priests lowered the mummy case into the stone sarcophagus by torchlight, a cruel ritual was performed before the entrance to the tomb. With a mighty blow a priest cut off at the tarsus the foreleg of a live calf that had been brought along in the mourning procession. Murals in the tombs repeatedly show such three-legged calves, but to this day we have no full explanation of the ritual's true significance.

Outside, in front of the entrance to the rock tomb, sacrifice priests occupied themselves with bulls and antelopes. These animals were thrown to the ground, their legs were tied together, and they were pulled by the tails. Two men tried to wring the neck of a bull, which they had grabbed by the horns; finally it crashed to the ground, and a priest pierced the animal's carotid artery with a huge knife; the gushing blood was caught in large bowls. Slowly life ebbed from the animal. Then it was the turn of the next one.

The practiced hands of the slaughterers began to carve up the animals—the stomachs were slit, the hearts were pulled out and shown to the crowd. "Come, you priest and wab, to this foreleg," one of the sacrificers called out, and the chief priest, the king's wab priest, drew near. He smelled the blood of the sacrificial animals, examined the meat with a critical eye, and then announced, "It is pure." Now the animals' forelegs were placed in the sacrificial fire, which was already blazing and sending up black clouds of smoke, and the workers at the sepulcher could begin to close the rock tomb for all eternity.

As it happened, eternity lasted for only a few brief decades. The records of the tomb robbers' trial during the twentieth dynasty mention the tomb of Amunhotep III as one that had been broken into.

When Amunhotep III died around 1365 B.C., Nefertiti's dowry had still not arrived in Thebes. Whether the cunning Tushratta had held it back purposely or whether the caravan had been plundered on its journey, we do not know. Given the Mitannian king's business acumen, however, and in view of the lavish dowry Tushratta had offered, we can assume that his calculations took into account the imminent demise of Amunhotep III.

In any case, shortly after Amunhotep's death the Egyptian envoy Khamassi arrived in Mitanni. (Khamassi is the Mitannian way of writing a name whose Egyptian form we do not know.) The envoy from Thebes brought the news that the son of Amunhotep III, Amunhotep IV, had ascended to the pharaonic throne and had chosen the widowed Nefertiti to be his royal wife (Tushratta already knew of the death of Amunhotep III).

This gesture raised Nefertiti from an insignificant secondary wife, whose only task was to be beautiful, to great
royal wife. And if for the present each of her steps was still
supervised by her mother-in-law, Tiy, this moment nevertheless marked the beginning of the few pleasant years in
her ever-changing life.

The mountains of Crete, the gardens of Persia, and the incense groves of Arabia brought their philosophy into his dreams, and the knowledgeable lips of Babylonia whispered to him of days long past.

—*Arthur Weigall*

5 | THE SUCCESSOR

Amunhotep III was buried. His successor was named Amunhotep IV. But even in Mitanni, Assyria, Khatti, and Babylonia it was common knowledge that Tiy was the true ruling force. The fourth Amunhotep—it was said—was still too young to rule the state. At the time he gained the throne he was about twelve years old. However, it can hardly be assumed that Tiy would have relinquished the power which she had held for almost ten years even if Amunhotep had been much older.

Some Egyptologists believe there is evidence that some years prior to his death Amunhotep III had installed his young son as co-regent. However, no official ancient Egyptian documents have been found to support this contention, and the few indirect references to a co-regency are open to interpretation. It is more reasonable to assume that Amunhotep IV had spent the major portion of his child-

hood and youth abroad; the successor to the mightiest
pharaoh so far was presumably intended, unlike his father,
to become familiar with even the most remote areas of the
realm. But these long stays away from home apparently
had served to estrange father and son considerably. Not
one picture shows the two of them together, not one text
names them in the same context. There are numerous family portraits showing Amunhotep III with his wife and
daughters, but Amunhotep IV never appears in them.
Even when his grandparents, Yuya and Tuya, died within
a few years of each other, the young Amunhotep IV was
not in Thebes, as the funerary gifts in their tombs prove.
Each member of the royal family left an offering—except
for the grandson and heir.

Where had Amunhotep IV spent his childhood? Among
other places, in Mitanni and in Palestine. Letters No. 29
and No. 116 of the Amarna correspondence indicate that
Amunhotep was acquainted with Nefertiti's father, the Mitannian king Tushratta, and the Palestinian ruler, Rib-
Addi. Since neither of those men ever set foot on Theban
soil, the young Amunhotep must have come to know them
in their homelands. In Amarna Letter No. 29, Tushratta
writes to Amunhotep IV:

> When my brother Nimmuria [Amunhotep III] had gone
> to his fate, the news was called out, and what was called I
> also learned. He was far away . . . and I cried on that day. In
> the middle of the night I sat; food and water I did not con-
> sume that day and I was in pain. . . . But when Naphuria
> [Amunhotep IV], the great son of Nimmuria by Tiy, his
> wife, the great one, wrote to me: "I shall carry out the royal
> rule," I spoke thusly: "Nimmuria is not dead." Now Naph-
> uria, his great son by Tiy, his great wife, has set himself in

his place, and he will truly not shift things from the place where they stood before.

How could Tushratta know that Amunhotep IV would not "shift things from the place where they stood before" if he had not heard this from the man himself? That Tushratta's letter is not simply a reply to a death notice from Amunhotep IV is apparent in the very first sentence, which clearly indicates that he had heard of the death only from an official courier.

Amunhotep IV must have met Rib-Addi just as he had met King Tushratta, for the tone taken by the vassal chieftain in Letter No. 116 points to a close acquaintance. Rib-Addi wrote to Amunhotep IV, "And see, the gods and the sun and Ba'alat of Gubla have given to you that you have seated yourself on the throne of your father's house in your land."

Surely Amunhotep IV learned and saw a great deal during his stay abroad. For one thing, he may have met the beautiful Princess Tadukhipa of Mitanni at an early age. And without question his universal education would have contributed to the broadening of his intellectual horizons. Perhaps it was even this early that the widely traveled Egyptian felt stirrings of doubt about the many gods, who were given different names in every country.

It may be considered certain that Nefertiti became queen of Egypt in the first regnal year of Amunhotep IV because the royal couple's first daughter, Meritaten, "beloved of the Aten," was born during the second year (probably 1362 B.C.).

But aside from the fact that it took place, we know practically nothing about the actual wedding of Nefertiti and Akhenaten. The marriage ceremony itself seems to have been completely meaningless among the ancient Egyptians. Some Egyptologists even believe that no such ceremony was ever held but that the woman simply moved in with the man, with wife and husband contributing one third and two thirds of the family fortune, respectively.

Nefertiti, the great royal wife at her mother-in-law's pleasure, lived as was fitting for the queen of a great empire. The eighteen-year-old had at her disposal an exchequer that would have made even the Queen of England green with envy. Her personal household alone, which Tushratta had sent to Egypt with her as part of the dowry, consisted of three hundred servants, including two chief nurses, two wetnurses, ten pages, thirty lady's maids, thirty manservants, and a hundred waiting women. In addition, Amunhotep was obliged to furnish at least an equal number of servants.

While Nefertiti and Amunhotep led a carefree life in the fairytale palace of Malkata, the bride's father in far-off Mitanni was less content with his fate. It galled Tushratta, greedy for gold, that now he was supposed to pay a second dowry for the same daughter. Therefore he wrote his young son-in-law a letter filled with reproaches. When he had sent the bridal gifts, Amunhotep III had apologized that they were not more splendid and promised many more following the bride's arrival in Thebes. Tushratta's messengers had seen with their own eyes that Amunhotep III had had golden statues cast, said to be intended for the king of Mitanni. But then death had come to the father, and Amunhotep IV sent inferior statues—wooden figures, merely studded with gold leaf. "I do not know," Tushratta wrote in a grieved tone, "how I came to deserve this."

To emphasize his displeasure, Tushratta utilized a proven method. He placed the two Egyptian couriers, Mane and Gilia, under house arrest in his palace—for just as long as it took the pharaoh to carry out his father's promise. The unpleasant task of bringing this piece of bad news to Thebes was assigned by Tushratta to two subordinate officials named Pirizzi and Tulubri, who started on their journey without any diplomatic gifts whatever—an outrage in those days. The king of Mitanni was making clear the extent of his anger.

Did all these happenings leave Nefertiti indifferent—or might she even have been the moving force behind the cat-and-mouse game? Whatever the reason, the two messengers from Mitanni were arrested as soon as they arrived at the Malkata palace of Thebes. For a few weeks nothing more happened; then Tushratta sent a letter in which he reminded Amunhotep IV of the friendship between Mitanni and Egypt. He, Tushratta, would return the seized couriers, Mane and Gilia, to Egypt immediately if the pharaoh would free Tushratta's messengers. Amunhotep replied with another reproach. Somewhere in Syria two men, crossing the frontier illegally, had violated sovereign territory—an offense that absolutely could not be tolerated. Their names were Artessupa and Asali. They had been brought before Nefertiti, who spoke their language, and after they had been interrogated, Amunhotep had expelled them across the border. Now he demanded that Tushratta punish them.

The notion cannot be dismissed that it was Nefertiti who pulled the strings for this sham duel. She had a good understanding of her father and his weaknesses, and she knew exactly how far it was safe to go. Tushratta promptly replied to the pharaoh that the two border violators had been punished but not killed, since Amunhotep had not insisted on the death penalty.

If we compare the letters Tushratta sent to Amunhotep III with those addressed to the pharaoh's son, Amunhotep IV, we are struck by the cordiality he extends to the former and the barely suppressed rage he expresses toward the latter. We must conclude that the young pharaoh had provoked the Mitannian king to the quick. If only Tushratta's position in his own realm had been a little stronger, a campaign against Egypt would not have been ruled out. As it was, the more or less well-concealed animosities were confined to the diplomatic correspondence, and we can imagine with what amusement Nefertiti and Amunhotep pounced on each new communication from his father-in-law.

Strange as it may seem, there is a distinct possibility that during the first few years of her marriage Nefertiti had to share her husband with her mother-in-law—that Tiy's relationship with her son may have gone far beyond the bounds of a normal mother-son relationship. Evidence for such a hypothesis has been found in the tomb of Yuya, the "Manager of the House, of the Great Dual Treasure House, and the Harem of the Great Royal Wife Tiy," with its unusually numerous and detailed wall pictures.

Yuya's tomb can be dated fairly precisely to the year 12 of the reign of Amunhotep IV. But although Amunhotep III had been dead for those twelve years, the tomb inscriptions still refer to Tiy, not only as "the mother of the king" and "the queen mother," but also as "great royal wife" and "great queen Tiy." In one depiction of the nightly enjoy-

*Tiy (left), Amunhotep IV (Akhenaten), and Nefertiti. Tiy's daughter Be-
ketaten stands next to her mother's chair. Two daughters of the ruling couple
can be seen near Nefertiti. (Drawing by Norman Davies from a tomb picture.)*

ment of a last beverage, Tiy sits across from her son. Nefertiti must be content with the place behind him.

The American psychologist Immanuel Velikovsky carefully examined Yuya's tomb and arrived at a provocative
theory about Beketaten, "the king's own daughter." To do
so, he used an astonishingly accurate rule of thumb of
Egyptologists, which says that, in depictions of children, all
who are the same size are about the same age. In Yuya's
tomb, Beketaten is depicted as the same size as Nefertiti's
third daughter, who was probably eight years old in the
twelfth regnal year of Amunhotep IV. But how can Beketa-

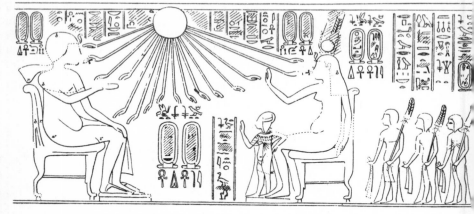

Amunhotep IV (Akhenaten), sitting at the left, greets his mother and wife, Tiy, as well as their joint daughter, Beketaten. Tiy and Beketaten raise their hands in a gesture of deference. (Relief on a lintel in the interior of the tomb of Yuya in Amarna drawn by Norman Davies.)

ten, "the king's own daughter" by Tiy, be only eight if her father, Amunhotep III, had been dead for twelve years? There is one convincing possible explanation—Beketaten is not the daughter of Tiy and Amunhotep III, but the issue of an incestuous union between Tiy and her son.

Finally, it is interesting to note that when Tiy died, Amunhotep IV had her laid to rest far from the tomb of her husband in the western royal mortuary valley near Thebes. In fact, he had her placed in his own tomb.

Sexual relations between mother and son were fairly rare in ancient Egypt—they were considered perverse. This seems strange, since the incestuous relationship between siblings and blood relations was considered quite legitimate. Nevertheless, a mother-son sexual union was taboo, and apparently at the court of Thebes and later in Amarna it was kept hushed up—especially from the populace, for whom the divine pharaohs could not set a bad example.

The relationship, however, could hardly be kept secret from the court and the foreign ruling houses that carried on a lively correspondence with Egypt. Thus the Babylonian King Burnaburiash (1370–1343 B.C.), writing to Amunhotep IV, calls Tiy "the lady of the house," supporting the conclusion that news of their union had already reached the land between the Euphrates and the Tigris.

Although we may never know the truth about Amunhotep's relationship with his mother, we know a good deal about that of Nefertiti and Amunhotep. As if they had known that the years of their happiness would be few, the couple tried to wrest from life only its most pleasant aspects. Nefertiti loved nature, such as the exotic fauna still found today on Kitchener Island in the Nile. Parks were established all over the city, studded with rare plants which slaves brought back from weeks of expeditions in the heart of Africa. Artificial ponds, intended to supply coolness and refreshment, were stocked with goldfish and ducks, Nefertiti's favorite animals.

During the first three years of her marriage Nefertiti gave birth to three daughters—Meritaten "beloved of the Aten," Meketaten "protected by the Aten," and Ankhesenpaten "living through the Aten." Nefertiti employed nursemaids, nurses, and a chief wetnurse—who supervised the others—to bring up her daughters.

Never before had a pharaonic couple carried on a family life that was as intense and demonstrative as that of Nefertiti and Amunhotep IV. When the two of them went for a ride in the golden chariot of state, their daughters invariably accompanied them. The children enjoyed an unusual amount of freedom in every way. They could be found anywhere in the royal palace and at any time; their presence was not a nuisance even when Amunhotep was engaged with officials on affairs of state. During the early years of their life together Nefertiti and Amunhotep also had no inhibitions about embracing in public and kissing—that is, rubbing noses.

The fact that Amunhotep was the ruler of a great empire and Nefertiti was mistress of Upper and Lower Egypt seemed a secondary consideration. Egypt was powerful and rich, and there were no political problems. Even should a crisis arise, it could simply be ignored.

Nefertiti knew how to guide the pharaoh with subtlety despite the critical gaze of her mother-in-law, Tiy. The young queen was at least five years older than Amunhotep, who seems to have been a delicate, somewhat sickly youth, practically begging to be mothered. The "lord of the sweet breath"—his epithet in early years—was chosen to rule a worldwide empire; but his universe consisted of the birds in the palace garden, the butterflies among the flower beds, the ducks in the rushes. He took little interest in politics; matters of state were left to his mother and his wife.

Apparently Tiy and Nefertiti had to maneuver the young pharaoh into public appearances, for there are hardly any portrayals in which we find Amunhotep alone. Tiy or Nefertiti—one or the other is always with him, most often Nefertiti. Pictures of the pharaoh without one of the two women, such as exist in the tomb of Ramose in Thebes, are an exception.

Ramose, vizier of Upper Egypt, began work on his tomb

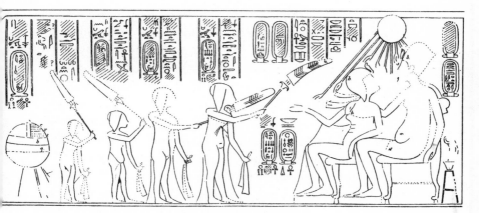

In this relief from Yuya's tomb, Amunhotep IV (Akhenaten) and Nefertiti are seated on thrones while four of their daughters fan them. (Drawing by Norman Davies.)

during the time of Amunhotep III and died before Amunhotep IV formally ascended the throne. Two reliefs, on either side of a doorway in the western wall of the great hall in his vault, show the young pharaoh, but in different ways. One relief depicts Amunhotep IV together with the goddess Maat. This portrait in the classical Egyptian relief style was clearly created immediately after the death of Amunhotep III. The relief on the other side was made somewhat later and unfortunately was never finished. Here we can already see the disk of the Aten with its armlike rays and Amunhotep IV in the typical new softer style, as well as Nefertiti, who, at the time this picture was made, was apparently still childless. Since the pharaoh's daughters always appear on later representations, we can date this relief to the first year of the reign of Amunhotep IV.

The Aten was, for the time being, nothing more than the

designation for the sun's disk. But the fourth Amunhotep perceived more in the golden, glowing, warming, life-giving sun. For him it was the divine, that which supported all—in short, the one god. Until recently most historians argued that Amunhotep initiated this turn to monotheism all by himself. But today such a thesis is no longer tenable. Since Nefertiti stood behind almost all governmental actions of the pharaoh, it is unlikely that the theosophical movement was brought to life by Amunhotep alone. The latest computer reconstructions of the gigantic temple of the Aten at Karnak prove precisely the opposite—the beautiful Nefertiti was a far more fervent adherent of the Aten faith than was her royal husband.

Judging by the scant evidence available from the early years of the reign of Amunhotep IV, the transition to the new religion was by no means abrupt. As we noted in chapter 2, the first surviving mentions of the sun god Aten occur during the reign of Amunhotep III, who, among other things, named his royal barge Splendor of the Aten. But at least throughout the early years of his rule, Amunhotep IV, like his father, continued to worship Amun.

Like many reformations, that of Amunhotep and Nefertiti began as unadulterated heresy. It did not introduce any revolutionary novelties but tried only to establish its differences from particular elements of the old faith. That Nefertiti played an important part in this process is beyond question, thanks to certain documents (to be discussed at greater length). We can easily imagine that from the outset the Mitannian princess felt suspicion and rejection of the confusing pantheistic cult of the Egyptians. And without a doubt the unprecedented action on the part of Amunhotep

III, who had ceased to trust his local gods and, hoping for a miracle, had asked that the Asiatic idol Ishtar be sent him, did not remain without consequences in Egypt. For the disowning of the animal-human Egyptian gods in favor of the rather abstract sun disk clearly embodies the mark of Nefertiti's cool intelligence. At the same time the rays of the sun disk, ending in hands, appear as a picture of naive belief in gods such as can be ascribed only to the young Amunhotep. Whenever the rays come near the faces of human beings, they hold the ankh, the symbol of life, before their noses for inhalation. The hands of the sunrays curl protectively around the royal crown or tenderly embrace the human body, quite like the old gods used to do.

As the German Egyptologist Heinrich Schäfer has shown, the "new" Aten symbol derived from old concepts. At the lower brim of the red-painted sun disk the emblematic cobra always sits with puffed-up head—just as on older representations of the sun—except that now the reliefs recall a motif seen earlier only in sculptures; the snake is moved to the center and faces front. Nor is there anything new about the humorous-seeming armlike rays of the Aten. Amun-Re had already been addressed in religious literature as "peerless one, many-armed."

If anything was basically new and different in the Aten faith, it was the concept of truth. That is why, when the fourth Amunhotep took the name Akhenaten, his epithet was "he who lives by the truth." The tendency of the deified Egyptian kings to return to the ground of reality was already noticeable in Amunhotep III; he had quite secular events, such as the hunt, immortalized on commemorative scarabs. This tendency became totally overt in the behavior of Amunhotep IV and Nefertiti, who kissed and embraced in public and took their little daughters even to state affairs. The burgeoning "Atenism" was therefore by no means in opposition to the traditional religion of the Egyptians—how else could it have been conceivable that the Aten temple of Karnak was simply an extension of the Amun temple?

In year 4 of the reign of Amunhotep IV, however, an event took place that was designated as something "bad" on one of the boundary stelae of Amarna. Because the ensuing text is unfortunately destroyed, we must rely on assumptions and speculations. It is highly probable that the "bad" event refers to a putsch of the Amun priests, who saw their own power waning with the decline of the old belief. Attempts on the part of these priests to enlist Nefertiti on their side had failed, so that in fact the last possibility of maintaining the old polytheism had been spent.

Nefertiti and Amunhotep countered the revolt, or whatever it might have been, with a rampage against priests, gods, tombs, and temples. The royal couple was supported by the fanatical masses, who suddenly saw themselves in the position of being able to take revenge against a priest class that had spread fear and terror among the people for centuries.

This Egyptian iconoclasm bore some strange fruit. Not only were geese—the animal holy to Amun—expunged from all wall reliefs and paintings, but even the hieroglyph for mother had to be erased from the old text and written from then on in a different way—because it so happened that the sign for mother and that for Mut, the wife of Amun, was the same. Scribes were charged with searching out and expunging the word Amun in the archives where the corre-

This line drawing from a painting on the southern wall of the tomb of Ramose depicts the four prophets of Amun. The names of the god Amun and his wife, Mut, were so defaced as to be unreadable.

spondence—written in cuneiform characters—with the kings of Babylonia, Khatti, and Mitanni was preserved.

Also in the fourth year of his reign, on the fourth day of Pharmuti (according to our calculations, in mid-January, 1360 B.C.), Nefertiti and her pharaoh rode northward to Amarna in their golden chariot of state. It was not the first visit for either of them. After careful consideration, they had decided to build the city of their dreams in this high valley, surrounded by rocky mountains to the east and the

Nile to the west—about two hundred miles from Thebes as the crow flies. On this bright spring day, when "the sky was in glee, the earth rejoiced, every heart laughed," the outward boundaries of the new royal city were to be staked out. It would be called Akhetaten—"horizon of the Aten."

It was not only that the famous head of Nefertiti was found here and that Tutankhamun began his reign here. It is already testimony enough of the unusual romanticism of a pharaoh if on a whim a royal city is founded on a previously uninhabited spot, is lived in and is destroyed again—a city which falls prey to the desert again after only a few years. And during its brief existence, this city was the capital of a great empire.

—*John D. S. Pendlebury,* Tell el-Amarna *(1935)*

6 | THE CITY OF DREAMS

When Nefertiti and Akhenaten arrived at the valley in their glittering chariot with the delicate six-spoked wheels, pulled by galloping, plumed horses, sacrificial fires were already sending up smoke from the rock altars. The forelegs of bulls and calves, birds, fruits, bread, beer, and incense, and all sorts of vegetables had been brought to the altars and piled up before the fires—offerings for the Aten as well as supplies for personal enjoyment. A true celebration had been planned.

The elite of the realm—officials, courtiers, and military leaders—had lined up in two rows by the time the young pharaoh and Nefertiti, who had wound her left arm around her husband's waist, brought the swift chariot to a halt. The king wore only a short leather loincloth; a delicate, diaphanous garment fluttered from Nefertiti's shoulders. Both were wearing their helmetlike crowns, somewhat

95

resembling leather headdresses—the kind familiar to us
from the famous bust of Nefertiti now in Berlin. While one
of the courtiers came running to help the beautiful queen
alight from the carriage, all the officials threw themselves
to the ground before the ruling couple and kissed the earth.
As Nefertiti descended, the courtier called out, "The great
crown princess in the palace, the beautiful and magnificent
one with the plumed crown, great in joy, who unites with
graciousness; rejoice to hear her voice; mistress of loveliness, great in being beloved, with whose existence the lord
of both lands is well pleased, the great one... of the Aten;
who gives satisfaction... in the horizon; to whom whatever
she speaks is granted [this formulation is extraordinary, indicating Nefertiti's power]; his beloved great royal wife, the
mistress of both lands Neferneferuaten Nefertiti, eternal
life!" (The text of this ceremony is found on a border stela
in Amarna.)

And the crowd repeated, "Eternal life!"

Then Akhenaten descended from the chariot while the
courtier, facing the crowd, called out, "The King of Upper
and Lower Egypt, the one who lives on truth, the lord of
both lands, Neferkheperure, unique one of Re, son of Re,
who lives by truth, lord of the crowns of Akhenaten, great
in his lifetime, eternal life!"

"Eternal life!" the crowd echoed.

While Nefertiti and Akhenaten approached a double
throne that had been erected under a canopy in front of the
altars, a servant ran to the pharaoh's golden chariot and
carried out the royal couple's two little daughters, Meritaten and Maketaten. In high spirits, they ran up behind
their parents and took their place on the steps to the throne
as if it were a matter of course.

Raising his left hand, Akhenaten spoke. "Let the servants of the king, the great ones in the palace, the chiefs of the army throughout the land be brought to me." And the summoned people stepped forward, cast themselves down before him, and touched the dusty ground with their noses.

"See," said the pharaoh. "Akhetaten was desired by the Aten. It shall be built as a memorial to his name in all eternity. It was the Aten, my father, who showed me Akhetaten. Not any official found it, nor any other person in all the land, that he would raise Akhetaten at this place, but the Aten alone, my father, found it, to build it for him as Akhetaten."

This form of expression, which appears clumsy to us, corresponded to the pharaoh's usual elevated diction. The several repetitions of ideas was nothing more than a way of emphasizing the statement. Akhenaten spoke while sitting; Nefertiti sat at his right, her left hand resting on his right forearm. This posture almost imparted the feeling of a family gathering to the highly official ground-breaking ceremony for the new national capital of Akhetaten.

Under Akhenaten's father, a similar situation would have been arranged as a feast with Oriental trappings, where the priests of Amun would still have sacrificed human beings—a handful of luckless slaves from the last campaign against Asia or Nubia. Something of the kind would hardly have occurred to the gentle young pharaoh. And another circumstance caught the eye: for the first time an official act of state was being conducted without Tiy's appearance. Observers of the scene at court were not surprised at this; they had already noticed for some time that the beautiful Nefertiti was increasingly taking Tiy's place.

In response to the king's speech, a cry of rejoicing went up from the people. The officials and chamberlains fell to

their knees and bowed down before the sun, which was
sending merciless, searing heat from the skies. Then they
intoned a carefully rehearsed litany, a hymn to the Aten,
which ended in a paean of praise for the pharaoh.

> You bring all lands to him, you make all cities pay tribute
> to him. All lands, all foreign lands and the distant north-
> men bring their offerings, in that their deliveries are on
> their backs for him who created life, through whose rays
> one lives and whose breath one breathes....

At a sign from Nefertiti, the pharaoh once more raised his
hand heavenward, and in a loud voice spoke to the people.
(The speech is reproduced on a boundary stela in Amarna.)

> As true as my father Re-Herakhte, which is the Aten, lives,
> I will build Akhetaten for the Aten, my father, in this
> place.... I shall erect the great Aten temple for the Aten,
> my father, in this place. I shall erect the smaller Aten
> temple for my father, the Aten, at that place. I shall erect
> the sunshade of the great royal wife, Neferneferuaten Nefer-
> titi, for the Aten, my father.... I shall arrange all the work
> at this place. I shall lay out estates for the pharaoh, and I
> shall arrange estates for the royal wife in Akhetaten at this
> place. My tomb is being made in the eastern mountains of
> Akhetaten, and there my funeral shall be made in the mil-
> lions of sed festivals which my father, the Aten, will com-
> mand for me, and in it shall be buried the great royal wife
> Nefertiti in these millions of years... and in it shall be bur-
> ied the princess Meritaten in the millions of years.
> If I die in a city to the north, south, west, or east in the
> millions of years, let me be brought and buried also in Ak-
> hetaten. If the great royal wife dies in a city to the north,
> south, west, or east in these millions of years, let her be
> brought and buried in Akhetaten. If the princess Meritaten
> dies in a city to the north, south, west, or east in these millions

of years, let her be brought and buried in Akhetaten. Further, let a necropolis be made of the Mnevis bull [incarnation of the sun-god Re in Heliopolis] in the eastern mountain of Akhetaten, and let him be buried therein. Let tombs be installed for the greatest of the prophets [high priests], the divine fathers of the Aten and the servants of the Aten. Let tombs be laid out for all officials and all the people in the eastern mountain of Akhetaten, where they shall be buried.

Akhenaten had completed his ceremonial address. He rose from his chair of state and came out from under the canopy into the bright sunlight. Slowly he approached the nearest of the stone offering tables and, assisted by two sacrificial priests, took the largest of the bulls' forelegs that lay ready in order to place it in the fire. Immovable, like a figure wrought from the white, translucent alabaster of Amarna, Nefertiti observed the performance from her seat under the protective canopy.

The ceremonies associated with the groundbreaking at Akhetaten lasted until late afternoon, when the sun was already low on the western horizon, casting long shadows across the golden-shimmering Nile.

So it was that in the year 1359 B.C., one hundred thousand technicians, engineers, and workmen began to build a dream city in a section of barren desert at the edge of the Nile, between Thebes and Memphis. It was to be a new capital of Egypt, a city that would have the most modern, most palatial structures, sufficient to house more than a hundred thousand people in an area that until then had hardly been penetrated by man. It was to be a city of the sun, of love, of art, and of joy, intended to realize mankind's age-old dream of a better, happier world. And it was the first city in the world to have been designed "on the drawing board," a feat that can be likened only to the modern-day Brasilia.

Originally, Akhetaten was supposed to occupy only the area between the Nile and the eastern mountainous region, but even as the first construction was going on at the eastern shore, the western shore became included in the plans. The erection of this desert city was a supreme achievement of ancient Egyptian technology, for aside from the material furnished by the huge alabaster quarries in the northeastern sector of Amarna, all building materials had to be hauled over hundreds of miles and prepared at the site. Before construction could actually begin, therefore, factories and workshops had to be set up, wells had to be sunk, and drainage ditches had to be dug.

Unlike his father, Akhenaten did not choose to build the foundations of his city from air-dried bricks of Nile mud. He used finely dressed ashlar, brought to Amarna from Upper Egyptian quarries by way of the river. We owe it to this fact alone that the foundations of most of the Amarna buildings are preserved to this day, so that we can reconstruct the actual buildings. Of course the tall structures were made, as they had been for centuries, of brick based on the air-dried Nile mud. This method of building seemed to be not only the cheapest but also the quickest. The delivery of the building material could take place promptly, there were no lengthy transports, and preparing the bricks was less expensive because it did not necessitate heavy sledges and complicated hoists. The only disadvantage of this material lay in the irregular shrinkage of the bricks during the drying process.

The architects of Akhetaten, therefore, used a traditional

system of hollow blocks that seems totally modern. In the first row, all bricks were laid lengthwise. In the next layer, the bricks, three to a row, were aligned along the short side. A hollow space resulted between the individual rows, allowing the air to circulate, and in this way the bricks dried as evenly as possible. To support the brickwork, wooden beams were drawn through in the manner of half-timbering. This lightweight architecture quite suited the nature of the new capital, but unfortunately it was far less resistant to the effects of weathering than were the monumental stone buildings. For this reason archaeologists had, and still have, a particularly hard time in Akhetaten.

On the thirteenth day of Peret in regnal year 6—the year that Amunhotep IV officially changed his name to Akhenaten, "serviceable to the Aten"—Nefertiti and the pharaoh once again rode the golden chariot from Malkata to Akhetaten to examine the progress being made on the city of their dreams. Because the entire area was still no more than one large building site, the couple resided in a tent called "the Aten is pleased." The access road to Akhetaten was apparently already completed, for the pharaoh made it very explicit that he took "the beautiful road"—the thoroughfare that was later to be known as the Royal Road. Finally, in 1357 B.C., a scant three years after construction had begun, the most beautiful city in the world and the new capital of Egypt was formally dedicated.

The principal street of Akhetaten, the Royal Road, ran from north to south parallel to the Nile, touching on all the city's most important buildings. A visitor to the city coming from Thebes to the south would first have passed a row of elegant private houses built along both sides of the

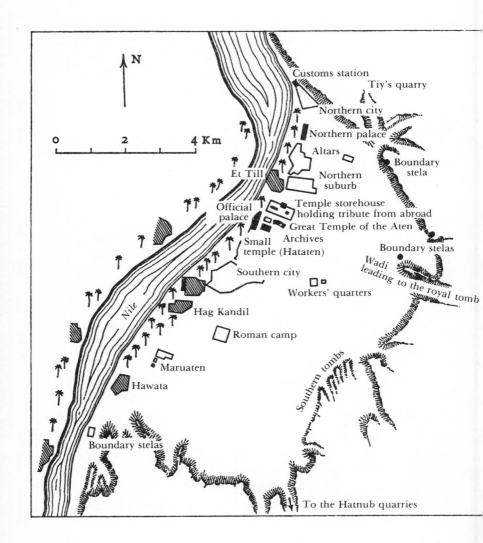

Akhetaten, the dream city of Nefertiti and Akhenaten on the Nile.

Royal Road. The well-to-do had built their homes, artful and splendid, along the city's other broad avenues also. The rubble and debris had been thrown on the properties lying behind the houses. Then less privileged people had come along, burned the rubbish and, using some of the debris at hand, built their houses in a second line, depositing the refuse in turn on the land behind *their* houses. This had been the signal for those entirely without means, who hoped for new beginnings in Akhetaten. Using the rubbish of the less propertied, the poorest had built meager huts in a third row—the world's first slums. Nefertiti and Akhenaten could not have seen them when they sped through Akhetaten in their golden chariot—no streets ran near them.

After passing the private homes along the Royal Road, the visitor would then have seen, to the right, the first great public building. It was the temple storehouse connected with a small sanctuary to the Aten. Across the way, on the left but not accessible from the road, rose the great pillared hall of the royal palace, where public audiences were held.

Continuing on, the visitor would pass under a covered bridge—the direct connection between the private rooms of the ruling couple, lying to the right of the street, and the official palace. Every morning, when Akhenaten and Nefertiti went from their living quarters into the court, the people thronged under the bridge to catch a glimpse of the beautiful queen. Window of Appearances is what the inhabitants of Akhetaten called the opening in the wall on top of the bridge where Nefertiti could be spied, often several times a day. And if the people called out her name and demanded to see her, she stepped to the window and waved while the populace cheered.

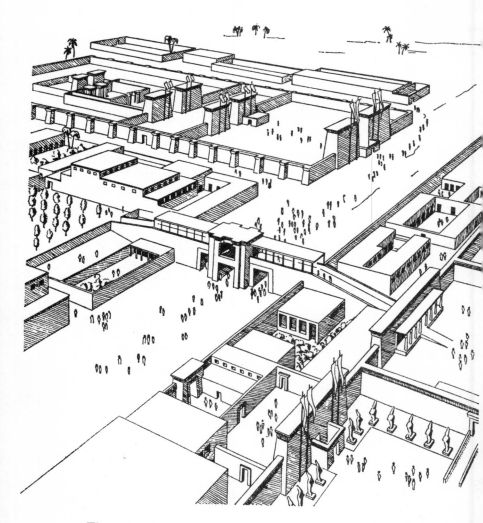

The town center of Akhetaten (now Amarna). The king was able to pass from the governmental palace (right) to the residence (left) by way of a covered bridge. He showed himself to the populace and distributed rewards from the central gallery. Judging by pictures in the Theban tombs, several of his successors followed his example. (Reconstruction of the town center, including the Window of Appearances, after Pendlebury.)

At the southern side of this high bridge an access ramp formed the official entrance to the king's personal apartments, which were slightly raised above the other buildings. Akhenaten, clasped tightly by Nefertiti, would rush upward in his golden chariot over this ramp into a great, parklike square, measuring about seventy yards square. Here the master of the horse and his stableboys waited to unharness the steeds, which were decked out in red feathers, and lead them away.

Around this park were grouped all the buildings that catered to the personal well-being of the royal couple. The most extensive space was required by the storehouses, where provisions, foodstuffs, and utensils were piled high. While such edibles as meat, fish, bread, and fruit were most often dried, vegetables and less perishable fruits had to be kept cool in dark, windowless underground chambers. Wine and beer, both of which the pharaoh enjoyed, were stored in thousands of pitchers.

From their apartments Nefertiti could pass unseen to the little temple whose main entrance faced the Royal Road. An altar stood at this entrance, flanked to the left and the right by offering tables. A pylon led directly to a second courtyard, and another pylon formed the gate to the Holy of Holies, which approximated almost exactly the one in the Great Temple. A line of trees was planted around the sanctuary; it was broken only on the south side by small buildings, whose purpose we do not know. A portrayal from the tomb of Tutu, which shows a temple encircled by an avenue, is possibly a reproduction of the Hataten temple.

In order to reach the private apartments on the south side of the park, several forecourts had to be crossed. A

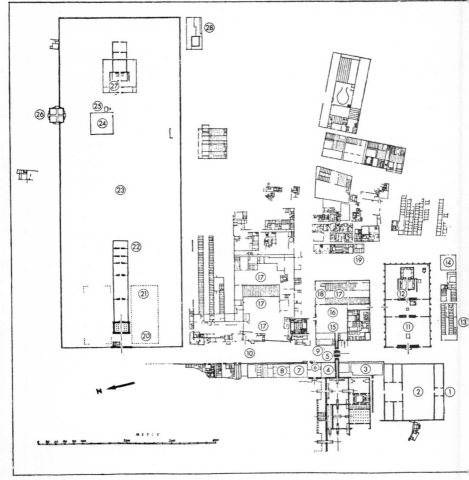

Survey Map of the Inner City of Akhetaten

1. Throne room
2. Great pillared hall
3. Storehouse
4. Southern harem
5. Window of Appearances
6. Courtyard
7. Northern harem
8. Garden
9. Bridge
10. Royal Road
11. Altar
12. Sanctuary
13. Temple storehouse
14. Lake
15. King's house
16. Garden
17. Storehouse
18. Pond
19. Archives
20. Perhai
21. Offering stones
22. Gematen
23. Great temple
24. Slaughterhouse
25. Stela
26. Hall Where
    Tribute Is Received
27. Sanctuary
28. Panehesi's house

portico of papyrus columns led to a hall with forty-two pillars, the living hall of the royal couple. Immediately after passing through this hall, the visitor would be standing once more in a light-suffused courtyard that formed the approach to the separate apartments of Nefertiti and Akhenaten. In contrast to many other ruling couples, they shared a large bedroom, which had side doors leading to a dressing room, a bath, and a separate toilet. Nefertiti's six daughters were quartered in a pavilion with six sleeping alcoves, situated somewhat to one side of the private chambers. This arrangement demonstrates that the queen did not personally see to her daughters' upbringing.

Yellow, the color of the Aten, predominated in all the rooms of the new royal palace. But if we recall the splendid palace at Malkata built by Amunhotep III, we can only say that his son's home, admittedly in good taste, was by no means furnished luxuriously. Though the walls and floors were painted with motifs from the world of butterflies, fish, and waterfowl, and though the capitals of the pillars glittered with gold and cut glass, Akhetaten nevertheless lacked the monumental pomposity preferred by Amunhotep the Magnificent. We cannot dismiss the impression that when the palace at Akhetaten was planned, the architect had some nebulous idea of a synthesis of nature and architecture.

The Great Temple of the Aten—275 yards wide and 800 yards long—lay at the exact center of the city along the Royal Road. This structure was intended to be the most magnificent building in the new city, the "house of my father the Aten, which I will construct in Akhetaten on this spot," the focus of the new faith. The surrounding wall, called Temenos, almost a mile and a half long, enclosed the holy ground which was to encompass several cultic buildings, according to the plans of Nefertiti and Akhenaten.

In order to get to the sanctuary of the Temple of the Aten, Nefertiti had to pass through a number of forecourts and pylons. All the buildings of the temple were roofless; facing the east, like the Early Christian churches, the place where the Aten was worshiped would offer easy access to the beaming sun. After she had left the large entrance gate behind her, the queen arrived in a huge pillared hall, the so-called Gematen, "the Aten has been found," a sequence of five pylons separated from each other by forecourts. To each side of the Gematen lay a festival hall, called Perhai, "house of rejoicing"; offering tables of stone were meant for the use of the people, who were not allowed to penetrate to the Holy of Holies.

Nefertiti had to go on another 325 yards to get from the Gematen to the sanctuary of the Aten, passing the slaughtering yard, a hall of fifty square yards where the sacrificial animals were killed. The sanctuary itself was also surrounded by a wall. After the entrance pylon, an avenue led to another surrounding wall, another pylon—and then a magnificent sight was vouchsafed to Nefertiti. To right and left of the sacred street, dozens of small altars were set up, leading straight to an imposing pillared hall. Four gigantic statues of the pharaoh had been erected between the monumental papyrus columns. The pillared hall bordered on the final and largest pylon in the Temple of the Aten, giving access to the forecourt of the sacred precincts. This was dedicated to the pharaoh's offerings to the Aten, in which Nefertiti also participated.

If the pharaoh ever felt shut in by the walls of Akhetaten, he drove along the Nile for a few miles to Maruaten, his small pleasure castle, which we must imagine to have lain across from the present-day village of el Hawata. Maruaten was entered through a great pavilion and a pillared hall. Past these was the throne hall, which had the appearance of an open veranda. Behind it an artificial lake—100 yards long, 50 wide—stretched out. A mooring quay of stone, decorated with reliefs, reached into three-foot-deep water afloat with flat skiffs. This lake was framed by a belt of trees and beds of flowers, among which roomy bungalows with sleeping, living, and eating apartments were set at random.

But by far the most spectacular structure in Akhetaten was the northern palace, reached by driving north along the Royal Road through several hundred yards of open country. If it had existed for only a little longer, the northern palace—Nefertiti's palace—would have been granted a worthy place in the ranks of the wonders of the world. Neither the palace of Knossos nor the hanging gardens of Babylon could compare with this architectural masterpiece, which managed to combine art and nature to a degree never before attained. Animal preserves and living quarters, ponds and flower beds—all seemed to form a single organic whole.

The center of the exotic ground plan was formed by a square lake from which two pillared halls led to a throne room. The north side was divided into three parts. An open court with a small sacrificial installation was adjoined by various animal preserves, and alongside stretched a park hemmed in by colonnades. The opposite side was also divided into three. Two building compounds served as refuges for servants and officials, and the third, in the southeastern corner, was part of Nefertiti's private apartments.

Actually the northern palace, with its animal preserves, aviaries, and fish ponds, was more like a zoological and botanical garden than a residence. Pictures of animals and plants decorated all the walls, floors, and ceilings of the building, which was flooded with light. Nature and art—one merged into the other.

The final and northernmost point of Akhetaten was formed by a great gate in a solid double wall. Behind this Nefertiti would subsequently retire to her own palace, which stretched all the way down to the Nile. The great House of the Watchmen, built in terraces down to the river, presumably also served as the delivery site for all goods.

In the mornings, when Nefertiti and her husband showed themselves to the people through the Window of Appearances, as well as at public audiences in the great pillared hall of the palace and in the temple, storehouses, and horsebarns, there was one man who seems to have been omnipresent—Ay. Whenever the pharaoh held open court for all who wished to submit any matter to him, Ay always carried the tall feathered fan. Originally designed simply to waft cooling breezes toward the master, the fan developed more and more, as time passed, into a symbol of power. The fanbearer became an important figure as a result of his constant presence at the pharaoh's official audiences.

Ay, "the beloved of his lord," held a dozen other offices, however, besides being "fanbearer at the right hand of the king." Among them were such important ones as Master of the Horse, which automatically also made him Supreme

The handsomest tomb in Akhetaten was that of Ay. Here, Ay and his wife Tey (bottom), showered with necklaces of "gold of honor," bow before the Window of Appearances, from which Nefertiti and Akhenaten continue to throw gifts.

Commander of the Cavalry and Supervisor of the Royal Cattle Reserves. Ay—whom Cyril Aldred believes to have been a brother of Tiy—bore the title God's Father, just as Yuya, Tiy's father, had when he held a similarly influential position under Amunhotep III.

If Ay was in fact one of Tiy's brothers, it is easy to understand his position of power, which he expanded steadily through the reigns of no less than three pharaohs, Amunhotep III, Akhenaten, and Tutankhaten (Tutankhamun). Furthermore, the wily old courtier was twice involved with pharaohs who were little more than children—Akhenaten and Tutankhaten. As the senior official and private secretary to Akhenaten, Ay was the gray eminence at the court of the pharaoh, and it is not surprising that as time went on, friction developed between him and Nefertiti, who also increasingly gained power and influence.

"I am," Ay said, "truly a righteous man, free of evil. My name comes to the palace because of its usefulness for the king and because of the hearing of his teaching, the doing of his laws, the not-changing of the words and not-damaging of the being." It may be that this statement is a self-justification on the part of Ay because of the open conflict between him and the queen.

It is surely no accident that during Nefertiti's lifetime Ay never achieved what must have been his secret goal—to become pharaoh of Egypt. After Akhenaten's death he came close to it, but for the time being he had to cede pride of place to Tutankhaten, Nefertiti's favorite. Only after the unexpectedly early death of the eighteen-year-old boy king, a few short years after Nefertiti's death, did Ay see his chance to capture the pharaonic throne.

Ay was miles above the other royal officials in rank. If any courtier came close to him in influence, it was Meriere, who bore the titles of Supervisor of Demons, Supervisor of the Treasury, Supervisor of the Royal Harem of the Great Royal Wife Neferneferuaten Nefertiti, may she live in all eternity, Royal Scribe Meriere, the Righteous Man. These, at least, are the epithets inscribed in his tomb in Amarna. What is left out of the inscription is his title of Greatest of the Seers of the Aten—high priest in the temple of the Aten. Unlike Ay, Meriere enjoyed Nefertiti's wholehearted affection.

The other court officials must also be mentioned, though none of them had any political influence: Pinhasi, Superintendent of Granaries of the Aten, Cattle Supervisor of the Aten, and First Servant of the Aten, who lived in a feudal residence near the Great Temple; Arennefer, butler to the court and supervisor of agricultural workers; Pentu, royal physician, chamberlain, and "royal scribe at the head of the king"; Tutu, the chamberlain; Mahu, lord over the Mazoi, the desert police housed in barracks at the edge of Akhetaten; General Ramose, who was out of work for all practical purposes; and Nakht, the vizier. Nakht took the office of vizier seriously, but despite his position as head of state, he was not able to determine policy. If he merits any kind of mention today, it is because he owned the handsomest private mansion in Akhetaten. Still less good fortune was enjoyed by Nakht's predecessor, Maia, whom the pharaoh abruptly sent into the desert. Only old Ani, a scribe, was able to make a name for himself by means of the numerous documents he manufactured.

All these men are known to us only through their artfully furnished tombs, which they had carved into the rock wall of the valley of Amarna. For politics was a secondary matter at the court of Akhetaten; religion and art took precedence.

Bek—a short, stout man, master sculptor to Amunhotep III—brought from the quarries of Aswan those ashlar stones out of which he chiseled the monumental figures of the royal couple that flanked the northern approach to the palace. The outstanding artistic personality of the epoch, however, was the master sculptor Thutmose, who maintained a whole building compound—with specialized workshops for stonecutters, plasterers, and molders—on the Street of the

High Priests. When his living, sleeping, and working quarters were excavated in the period 1912–13 by Ludwig Borchardt, everything was still in such good condition that
Borchardt could take samples from a pile of plaster that
Thutmose had had delivered to use on subsequent work.
Paints, palettes, chisels, drills, and other tools of the artist
can be examined today in the Berlin Museum.

Akhenaten personally instructed his master sculptor in
the new art style he had initiated, which had as its under-
lying principle maat—truth. Forgotten were formalism and
stylization; realism was the new law. In this context Walther Wolf has noted:

> That the king suddenly determined on a break with the
> past is shown most clearly by more-than-life-size statues,
> leaning against pillars, from a sanctuary he built to the
> Aten in Karnak. For while at the very outset of his reign he
> accepted the usual royal image, he now shifted to represen-
> tation of repellent ugliness, which shows him with a thin
> face, thick lips, swollen belly, and fat thighs. We sense that
> he rejected the style of his father as one representing empty,
> dull beauty and strove to lend strong expression to the ex-
> ploding emotional tensions.

The elongated skull and protruding chin were stylistic elements that influenced even pictures of the beautiful Nefertiti, at least during the early years of Akhenaten's reign.
The famous bust of Nefertiti, therefore, which may have
been created between regnal year 8 and regnal year 10, can
not be understood either as a simple aesthetic protest on
the part of master sculptor Thutmose or as a reverential
bow to the woman's beauty.

Nefertiti's influence on the art of Akhetaten can be de-
tected in a detail that has received little attention until

now. For centuries Egyptian artists shaped male statues with one leg extended forward—as if to express activity—while the female statues were always shown with legs parallel and closed. It is otherwise with the statues from the Amarna period; Akhenaten stands with closed legs, while Nefertiti extends one foot.

Maat—"truth"—for the first time in Egyptian art the models' ages can be seen; for the first time the work of art expresses pain, sorrow, joy. The severe system of coordinates vanishes, and the strictly symmetrical progression of adjacent figures dissolves in a variety of movement heretofore unknown. Incipient attempts are even made to employ perspective in two-dimensional mural painting.

Equally revolutionary are the motifs of the new style in art—no son of Re had ever before revealed such a human, private side of himself to his subjects. At first it must have seemed shocking when, hewn out of precious stone, a royal child's birthday party offered itself for admiration. But the populace became used to it and eventually even began to identify with these pictures. Where was the difference between their own family life and that of the divine pharaoh?

If an audience was held early in the morning, the pharaoh sat on his throne, the beautiful Nefertiti beside him, and on her lap the little princesses crawled and squirmed, as is shown by the fragment of a relief excavated by Flinders Petrie in Amarna. It is unfortunate that the limestone statue of the "kissing king" from the workshop of Thutmose, which Borchardt hid during the digging season of 1912–13 and which shows Akhenaten holding his daughter in his lap, was never completed. Tenderness was a central concept in Akhetaten art. Akhenaten caresses Nefertiti's chin; Nefertiti places a collar of woven flowers around the pharaoh's neck.

Much space was also given to depictions of the royal family's meals, including scenes of drinking; the paintings and reliefs in the tombs of Yuya, the royal physician Pentu, and the palace overseer Ahmose are good examples. And time and again we see the royal family on walks in the parks and on the garden terraces (tomb of Parennefer), as well as on drives in the golden chariot (tombs of Mahu and Ahmose).

For the first time the wife of a pharaoh appears on the war chariot, for the first time a woman is portrayed vanquishing the enemy. These motifs, however, should not be interpreted as an expression of the new style in art but rather as a sign of the extraordinary position enjoyed by Nefertiti.

Soft, flowing lines are the most obvious stylistic trait of Amarna art, which tended toward exaggeration and distortion until around the eighth year of Akhenaten's reign. The veiled look, often characteristic of the figures of this epoch, is brought about by omission of the lower eyelids.

Another novelty is the use of various materials in a single work of art. A head of Queen Tiy, only about four inches high, found in the ruins of Fayyum, is made of ebony and faced with stucco, and further enhanced with gilded linen and paste glass. The well-known painted limestone bust of Nefertiti in Berlin is stuccoed with plaster over a raw limestone core and thus cannot be said to be made from a single material. Modeling in plaster was a skill that was rediscovered in Akhetaten and raised to a new art form. As finds in the Teti pyramid in Sakkara clearly show, death masks had been made as early as the sixth dynasty. During the Amarna period, on the other hand, plaster casts of living

Nefertiti embraces Akhenaten, who steers the chariot of state with a sure hand, while Meritaten leans across her father's quiver in order to spur on the horses. (Norman Davies's restoration of a damaged ink drawing from the tomb of Ahmose in Amarna.)

persons were made. With this technique, eyes and facial wrinkles were inserted later. For the bust of one unidentified old man, the artist—presumably Thutmose—scratched in delicate lines that radiated outward at the outer corners of the eyes. Additional work on the stucco head was necessary if for no other reason than that the original impression was made without first creaming the face, so that when the plaster was removed, inaccuracies inevitably resulted and important details were wiped away. The reason the models' faces were not covered with ointment remains a mystery; instead, thin linen swatches or dampened papyrus was used as a protective layer—at least that is the conclusion we must draw from the odd pleatings found at the edges of the hair or under the chins of the masks. For the sculptor these stucco heads were primarily the required realistic models for subsequent sculpting in other materials.

The new style created by Akhenaten and Nefertiti aspired to more than merely a revolution in the arts. There is no doubt that, according to Walther Wolf in *Das alte Ägypten,* it was designed to "realize their new world view and be used as a means of religious propaganda." For thousands of years the Egyptians had worshiped a multitude of gods. And now there was to be only one.

As we have noted, Nefertiti and Akhenaten were undoubtedly happy in the early years of their marriage. But by the fourth year of Akhenaten's reign, when he was just sixteen years old and Nefertiti twenty-one, he had already begun to undergo a strange transformation.

Relief pictures in the tombs and on the boundary stelae of Akhetaten reveal anatomical anomalies in the pharaoh that apparently also affected his personality. Akhenaten's head became increasingly enlarged, and as his arms and legs grew more spindly, his chest, hips, and thighs seemed to swell. As the disease progressed, the contrast between Nefertiti and Akhenaten grew more pronounced—she, the most beautiful, most lovable queen the country had ever possessed; and he, the most grotesque, pitiful pharaoh who had ever ruled over Upper and Lower Egypt. Nefertiti, however, did not allow herself to be deterred by her husband's appearance. On the contrary, it seems that initially the pathological changes in Akhenaten aroused in her those maternal feelings that the young pharaoh so much needed.

Although they may never be certain, the majority of scientists diagnose Akhenaten's disease as hydrocephalus. This disease is not a single, clearly definable disorder but rather a symptom or a cause of various clinical syndromes. Furthermore, neurologists have discovered that hydrocephalus can be an indication both of idiocy and of above-average intelligence.

In the opinion of Dr. Hans E. Kehrer, a psychiatrist and neurologist, people with a hydrocephalic skull structure evince abnormal traits in their psychic and social behavior. In addition, they tend to be small in stature, and their life expectancy is short. All these symptoms may appear simultaneously, but one or the other can just as easily be absent. On the other hand, the clinical picture usually reveals that only single modes of behavior and abilities are disturbed or stressed. An extraordinary degree of emotional irritability is also considered a typical hydrocephalic symptom.

Excitability and irritability often have their origin in very severe, almost unbearable headaches, and these in turn frequently lead to vomiting. If we look at the works of art of the Akhetaten period on the basis of this knowledge for once, we become aware of a very specific motif, which Egyptologists have not credited with any great significance. At the time of Nefertiti, there appears the first representation in Egyptian art history of people vomiting—a phenomenon that disappears again after that period. Could it be that the vomiting disease of the ruler had so involved his people that it was even portrayed in their art?

Nefertiti's husband, then, was ill from the time he was sixteen and gradually developed into a pitiful thing, dependent on the support and intellectual enterprise of a strong personality—his wife. "Aside from impairment of intelligence," according to Kehrer, "other psychic functions often undergo alteration with hydrocephalus. In thirty-three of our own patients with severe ventricular enlargement, who were examined extensively for psychopathology, we found lack of energy, listlessness, apathy, states resembling depression, and occasionally also foolish euphoria, persistent hyperactivity, and erethismus [a condition of heightened excitability], here too without a direct connection between the severity of the symptoms and the degree of hydrocephalus."

In the 1950s British and French neurologists realized that the appearance of hydrocephalus in adolescence is also connected with sexual impairment. In the case of Akhenaten, there is no doubt that he suffered from retrogression or malformation of the genital organs. A statue of him, preserved in Cairo, shows the pharaoh naked, without any male sex organs at all.

In addition to whatever effect Akhenaten's disease might have had on his mind, his psychic constitution also may have been deeply marked by hatred of his father. Karl Abraham, one of the outstanding students and co-workers of Sigmund Freud, dealt with the problem of negative relations between Akhenaten and Amunhotep III in his *Psychoanalytic Studies*.

> A look at the history of many a family lets us note how a strong personality emerges from the group and breaks new ground by his activity. Even the son of such an outstanding

man already may begin the decline of the family. Frequently the son lacks the vigorous constitution of the father. But even if he does inherit it, he nevertheless grows up in the shadow of an overly powerful personality and is thus prevented from developing freely. He continues the work of his father without topping the older man's success. His need for power shows itself in his aggravated demands on life, in an inclination to pleasure and luxury. The next generation then tends to be even more lacking in energy and enterprise, turning instead to excessive fastidiousness and to sentimentality. Unable to meet the demands of reality, these family members head toward neurosis.

This is exactly what happened to Akhenaten. His whole short life was an unremitting attempt to free himself from dependence on his father. The young man could not help but see his father as the quintessence of power and potency—after all, his successes in the hunt were as phenomenal as his harem was large. Furthermore, his father possessed the one human being to whom the entire libido of the young Amunhotep was directed—his mother, Tiy. Toward the older man he could feel only impotent enmity and jealousy.

The fatal aspect of the young pharaoh's situation is that Tiy was far superior in intelligence and enterprise to her husband. Since, however, in Tiy this cleverness and energy were also paired with beauty, to which the son was particularly receptive, the necessary process of cutting loose from his mother was made infinitely more difficult.

Karl Abraham points out that, in cases such as this, the separation often fails entirely. Even when it is successful, it remains incomplete, and there is a compensatory tendency to similarly reattach oneself exclusively to one other person.

"The transfer of the libido, once accomplished," Abraham writes, "tends to be final and irrevocable."

And this process applies precisely to Akhenaten. We do not know whether it was his personal wish to marry his father's seventeen-year-old widow or whether Tiy deliberately promoted or even insisted upon the union. We are certain, however, that it was she who determined matters of state during the first few years of the young pharaoh's reign, as we are sure that in the early years of his marriage Akhenaten literally showered Nefertiti with affection. It may be that the fact of marrying his own stepmother and in this way taking something away from his father gave him a certain satisfaction; the actual confrontation with the overly powerful father figure, however, ran its course on another level.

The strongest tradition, which set the tone for everything else in ancient Egypt, was religion. Akhenaten broke with it, conferring on the Aten—the "new," singular god—a kind of authority never possessed by any of the gods before him. Art was equally linked to tradition. The young pharaoh introduced a revolution in aesthetics, in which traditional idealism was turned into realism, even a kind of expressionism.

No matter how many negative traits can be ascribed to Akhenaten, one fact cannot be disputed: he was a pacifist. And this was not out of indolence, as it was for Amunhotep III, but from conviction. Not only did he do away with the practice of human sacrifice, which was still common during his father's lifetime, he may even have abolished capital punishment. In any case, no reports of executions exist from the time of his reign. Unlike his father, he loathed hunting, the pastime of the rich. While countless wall paintings from the era of Amunhotep III tell us of duck hunts and fishing expeditions, under Akhenaten painted animal scenes take on a much more peaceful cast. In these, the little fishes leap merrily in the waters, and the ducks flit quacking through the reeds. But at the time he commissioned these works from the finest artists in the realm, he was not yet marked by his severe illness. Soon it would begin to cause serious problems between him and the beautiful Nefertiti.

7 / THE DISCORD

Valley of the Kings, near Thebes, 1907. The American archaeologist Theodore M. Davis discovered the ruins of a tomb here (later assigned the number 55 in the Theban tomb catalog) that he believed to be the final resting place of the royal mother, Tiy. But after exhaustive tests, six other archaeologists declared the mummy to be Tiy, Akhenaten, Nefertiti, someone named Smenkhkare, or an unknown person.

The following facts should enable us to make a more precise identification today.

1. The mummy is that of a man who was about twenty years old when he died, according to anatomical studies.

2. A gold leaf found in the coffin bears the epithet "beloved of Uaenre."

3. The cobra, the sign of royal power, is found on fragments of the coffin.

124

4. The mummy holds the royal scepter.

5. The tomb contains seals with the cartouche of Tu-tankhamun, indicating that the burial must have occurred during his reign.

These five facts fit only one of the four named persons: Smenkhkare, a man who may be the most mysterious figure in all of Egyptian history. At his death, Smenkhkare was barely twenty years old; Akhenaten had bestowed Nefertiti's epithet, "beloved of Uaenre," on him and had named him co-regent. Smenkhkare would therefore have been entitled to hold the royal scepter, and he might very well have been buried only when Tutankhamun had already ascended the throne.

Smenkhkare was the man who sealed Nefertiti's fate. No woman ever dared compete with her—it had to be a man who stole her husband and drove her into exile.

Who was this ominous personage named Smenkhkare? Egyptologists have put forth widely diverging theories to explain his origins, including that he was the brother of Tutankhamun; he was the son of Amunhotep III by an unknown secondary wife or by his own daughter, Sitamun; he was Akhenaten's son.

Whoever Smenkhkare was, he had an unusually close relationship with Akhenaten. Various pictures show such scenes as Akhenaten tenderly stroking his co-regent's chin, or Akhenaten and Smenkhkare in an intimate tête-à-tête at the dinner table, or Akhenaten and Smenkhkare together with Nefertiti's daughter Meritaten. The fact that Smenkhkare married Meritaten raises the question of whether the marriage was concluded for political and tactical reasons or because Akhenaten, harboring homosexual tendencies and somewhat mentally unbalanced from his disease, wished to place Smenkhkare close at hand.

Perhaps Smenkhkare himself was bisexual. It is even possible that Akhenaten actually regarded his male co-regent as his wife. One support of this hypothesis is the position of the arms of Smenkhkare's mummy, which corresponds to that of a *female* royal mummy—left arm across the chest, right arm stretched along the body.

Because on November 21, 1352 B.C., a great festival was held in Akhetaten in which the pharaoh and his queen together received the tributes of the vassal nations, we know that as late as the twelfth regnal year the couple was still actively sharing their lives—at least as far as outward appearance was concerned. Was it a unique, spectacular event that ultimately drove them apart, or did the king and queen become estranged little by little?

As we conclude from various finds, the latter is the case. Gradually the royal family, as well as the court and the officials, were split into two camps. There were followers of the beautiful queen and followers of the sick pharaoh. Thus we find in the northern palace, which Nefertiti later inhabited alone, some records relating to Akhenaten that mention Smenkhkare and Meritaten—but make no reference to Nefertiti.

We get additional clues from so-called wine-jar dockets. The Egyptians customarily sealed wine in large jars and provided each with a stamp indicating the vintage, using the name of the current pharaoh and the year of his reign. Such dockets found in the northern palace bear the name of Nefertiti only, a most astonishing fact, since wine-jar

This small tablet (Stela 17 813, about 8 inches high) arouses the passions of Egyptologists. Is the person depicted on the left Nefertiti or could it be her rival, Smenkhkare?

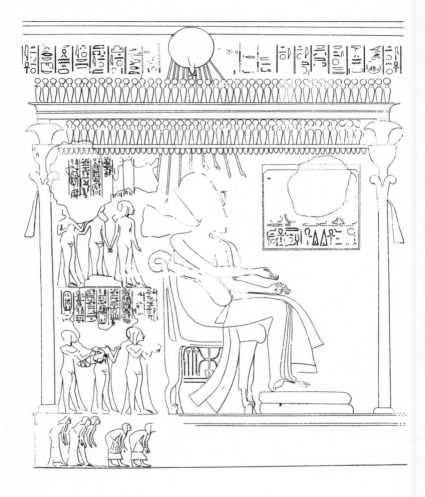

Akhenaten and Nefertiti (visible in the double profile of Akhenaten) at the great reception that took place in year 12 of Akhenaten's reign. Their six daughters stand behind them. (Drawing by Norman Davies from a wall relief in the tomb of Meriere in Amarna.)

seals in every other instance give the *pharaoh's* regnal year. The sole mention of Nefertiti leads to the conclusion that she no longer recognized her husband as the ruler.

No later than the year 1351 B.C., therefore, we are dealing with two family parties. On the one side stands Nefertiti, on the other Akhenaten with Smenkhkare and Nefertiti's oldest daughter, Meritaten. Though the second-oldest daughter, Meketaten, was also drawn into these intrigues, she died before the final separation took place. Ankhesenpaten, the third daughter, was still too young to take sides and did not take her place alongside her father until later. We know practically nothing of the position in the family feud of the three younger daughters, who were from two to seven years old.

Now that the conflict had come into the open, nothing was allowed to remain that could recall Nefertiti. Her name was never to be mentioned in public from that time on. Wherever it appeared in murals and reliefs, it was painted over with color, spackled over with plaster, or chipped away with a hammer. The name of her daughter Meritaten was inserted into her cartouches.

Though Meritaten was not a great royal wife, she was a queen. This status was publicly proclaimed and announced in the diplomatic notes as well. Beginning with year 14 of Akhenaten's reign, the documents of the Akhetaten correspondence no longer mention the great royal wife but only the queen—that is, Nefertiti's daughter Meritaten.

Outwardly Nefertiti continued to be the untouchable beauty. Her double life took place behind the high walls of her palace in the northern city, where—only a few miles away from her husband Akhenaten and his favorite,

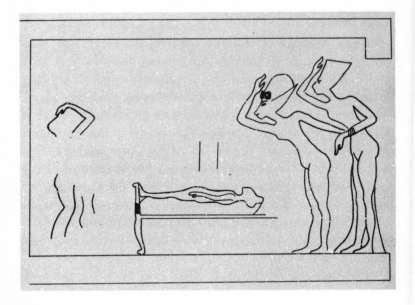

Akhenaten and Nefertiti grieving over the body of their little daughter Meketaten.

Smenkhkare—she held court, guarded by her personal police escort.

One man who frequently visited her in her palace was the master sculptor, Thutmose. No queen of the New Kingdom was so often, so artistically, so handsomely portrayed as Nefertiti. We can make this claim even though only the smallest part of Nefertiti's portraits escaped the hatred of her husband and the vandalism of the later pharaohs Horemheb and Ramesses II.

Surely the beautiful Nefertiti felt flattered when the court sculptor arrived each month granted by the Aten to the world, equipped with drawing reed or hammer, chisel,

The Colossi of Memnon, monolithic statues of crystalline quartzite about 60 feet tall. They represent Amunhotep III.

Akhenaten, Nefertiti, and her daughter Meritaten sacrificing to the Aten. (Limestone relief from the great palace of Akhetaten in the National Museum, Cairo).

Ay (right) as pharaoh performs the ritual of the opening of the mouth on Tutankhamun, who survived Nefertiti by a very few years and who appears here in the guise of the death god Osiris. (Picture from the tomb of Tutankhamun in western Thebes.)

Above: Ankhesenamun and Tutankhamun. (Portrait from the backrest of a throne chair from the late Akhetaten period in the National Museum, Cairo.)

Below: Akhenaten (left) and his co-regent Smenkhkare. (Limestone relief from Amarna in the National Museum, Cairo.)

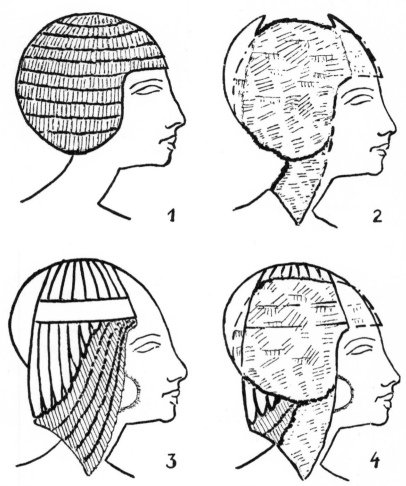

Nefertiti was displaced by her own daughter, Meritaten, on many reliefs, by the artists commissioned by Akhenaten, as follows: Nefertiti's head (1) was treated with a chisel to achieve a rougher ground for the application of new material (2). Plaster—a material generally popular during the period—was used to form the hairstyle typical of Meritaten (3). Today these alterations are discovered by softening and removing the top layer so we can see the superimposition of Meritaten's head on Nefertiti's (4).

and plaster to make a new sketch, a new sculpture, or a new model bust. There are no documents to prove what follows, but the hypothesis does not lack a certain basis in fact. Thutmose was ravished by the beauty of his queen, not only as an artist but also as a man. After all, he saw the rejected wife of the pharaoh more often than anyone else; he depicted her nude, he made casts of her head and neck. One is inclined to say that if in the course of these visits he did *not* fall in love with this woman, then he was not a man.

And yet even Thutmose seems to have been sent away or dropped. The missing left eye of the otherwise perfectly wrought bust of Nefertiti may be interpreted as the expression of impotent revenge on the part of the artist against his fickle beloved.

The fact that Nefertiti lived apart from the pharaoh in the northern palace shows not only that they were in conflict but also that Nefertiti clearly planned a coup d'état. For if she had been concerned only with separating from Akhenaten, she could easily have avoided him by living in Thebes or Memphis. But she wanted to remain in Akhetaten, the new capital.

Nefertiti probably lacked no luxuries and was in no great bodily harm, but she must have seethed with rage against Smenkhkare. This was the man who not only had robbed her of her husband but who also posed a serious threat to the Aten religion, which she embraced with all her heart and soul. Smenkhkare was more strongly attracted to the old polytheism of the Egyptians, and no doubt he knew how to draw the unstable Akhenaten to his side. The pharaoh may also have realized the difficulty of converting the Egyptian people, who had brought offerings to their local gods for thousands of years, to the one great god. Furthermore, the corrupt Amun priesthood had still not lost its influence over the masses.

Smenkhkare did not wish to remain in Akhetaten. It was his plan to move back into the national capital of Thebes when he took over sole rule. As we learn from an inscription in the tomb of the Amun priest Pawah (Number 139), in the third year after his ascension to the throne Smenkhkare began to build a mortuary temple of his own in Thebes. It was never completed, however, for the young coregent died quite unexpectedly.

It is very likely that Smenkhkare succumbed to a plague that at the time was raging in the Near East and had spread to Egypt by caravan. The Amarna letters refer to the plague repeatedly. The Cypriot king complains that "Nergal has killed the people," that his own son has died of it, and that hardly anyone is left to work in the copper mines. A Babylonian princess allegedly intended for Akhenaten died of the plague before she could even begin her trip to Egypt.

Then, in the seventeenth year of his reign, Akhenaten—his body wasted from disease, his mind destroyed—died as well. Suddenly all problems seemed solved, and Nefertiti dared to hope again.

You let me find grace before the king, each day and unendingly, and gave me a beautiful burial at the end of old age in the rock wall of Akhetaten, after I had beautifully brought my lifetime to a close as servant of the great god. No matter where he went, I followed close on his heels. He raised me when I was still a child until in peace and joy I attained the dignity of serving the ruler so that he was always happy.

—Wall inscription in the tomb of the fanbearer to the right of King Ahmose

8 / THE END

As we know from tomb inscriptions, Smenkhkare had begun to build a temple to Amun in Thebes. And though the pet names with which Akhenaten showered Smenkhkare only begin to indicate the influence the latter exercised over the pharaoh, we can imagine that the days of the Aten were numbered in Akhetaten.

Nefertiti had passed the final four years before Smenkhkare's death alone and in retirement. Only a few people in the country were even aware that the beautiful queen, the idol of an entire generation, was still alive. Though no official notice of her death had ever been broadcast—unless we count the fact that her cartouches were destroyed everywhere—neither was there any indication that she was still alive. Only the highest officials and the court knew about her exile. For almost five years no monument had been constructed that bore her image or even her name. The process of obliterating her memory continued inexorably.

134

Her cartouches were still being chipped away and replaced by those of her daughter Meritaten.

When Akhenaten died, Nefertiti was thirty-four years old. And as suddenly as she had vanished from the political arena, she was able to come to terms with this new situation. There she was once again, an intelligent woman, respected equally by friend and foe, acting more quickly and cleverly than the men around her could believe. Nefertiti's wine-jar dockets—discussed in the preceding chapter—hint at the possibility that in the confusion of the late Akhetaten period the beautiful queen herself ruled as the pharaoh, since the dating of the wine-jar dockets refers only to the period after Akhenaten's regnal years.

One of Nefertiti's first acts was to dictate to her scribe a letter to King Suppiluliumas of the Hittites, and the exchange of messages that followed must be one of the most famous in all world history. For many years it was believed that the sender of the messages was Ankhesenpaten, Nefertiti's third daughter, who was married, for unknown reasons, by her father—or, more probably, stepfather—Akhenaten shortly before his death. For the documents, translated into Akkadian, were signed only "Dahamunzu"—the queen. However, such leading Egyptologists as the American Donald B. Redford, an expert in the chronology of the eighteenth dynasty, consider Nefertiti to have been the sender.

We know about the exchange of letters only through the annals of the Hittite King Suppiluliumas, which were written down by his son Mursillis II and found in the clay-tablet archive of Boghazkeu. Herewith the wording of Nefertiti's first letter.

> My husband is dead and I have no son. The people say

that your sons are grown up. If you will send me one of
your sons, he will become my husband, for I do not wish to
take one of my subjects to make him into my husband.

Dahamunzu

This letter raises the question of the reason for Nefertiti's
wishing to marry a prince from Khatti, of all places. Border skirmishes, especially in the area of the northern Egyptian province of Syria, had produced a fairly tense
relationship between the two countries. And yet we are
asked to believe that Nefertiti, who had once been so
proud, should beg for one of the sons of the enemy, and one
she did not even know?

Nefertiti had her reasons. Never before during the period
of the eighteenth dynasty had Egypt seemed so built on
sand. Reformation and counterreformation had split the
land into two camps. The political incompetence of Akhenaten and Smenkhkare had aroused discontent in even
the lowest stratum of the population. If the rulers of neigh-
boring empires had not been equally at odds, if the chaotic
conditions in their own countries had not required all their
energies, then a single campaign, a single battle (though
matters would probably never have gone so far) would
have sufficed for Egypt to cease to exist in 1300 B.C., and
the history of the world would have run a different course.

But no battle erupted, no campaign against Egypt was
initiated. Nefertiti did not know whether the number of
her followers among the people was still sizable, she knew
only that the greater part of the army stood on the side of
her late husband. If she opted for an adherent of her own
religion, the choice would have resulted in a revolt of the
newly strengthened Amun priesthood, which was backed

by great sections of the army. But if she chose a pharaoh who was loyal to Amun, he might well have used his formal powers for Amun and against the Aten.

Nefertiti was not concerned with her personal happiness, she cared about rescuing a particular policy, a particular religion. She therefore decided on a step that was highly unusual for a woman at that time—she advertised for a husband. If Suppiluliumas agreed, then, she knew, Egypt would not only have overcome her most severe crisis, she would even constitute a new superpower, a universal empire, a worldwide ruler. Most especially, however, she must have hoped that a pharaoh of Babylonian origin would be the best guarantee for the continuation of the Aten faith. And in any case, one thing she considered certain: with a Hittite royal prince on the throne of the pharaoh, no war would ever break out between Egypt and Khatti. Nefertiti set out on the escape into the future.

But why did she not call on her father, Tushratta, or some Mitannian prince, one of her brothers, for help? Because matters were even worse in Mitanni than in the other countries. Tushratta's sons were estranged from each other, and one of them eventually killed his father. Presumably Nefertiti had never even met her blood brothers, since they cannot have been born until after she had gone to Egypt. And since the surviving documents contain none that mentions a visit by Nefertiti to her old home, we can assume that for all practical purposes she had broken off relations with Mitanni.

On the one hand, Nefertiti's lines to Suppiluliumas express the fear of gambling away her last chance; on the other hand, however, we cannot ignore the self-assurance and pride implicit in her emphasis on her distaste for marrying one of her subjects.

King Suppiluliumas's immediate response was confusion. His two generals, Lupakkis and Tarhuntazalmas, had just taught Egypt a rather crude lesson. In Amki (near the present-day Turkish city of Antakya), in the border region, they had made mincemeat of everything in sight and taken captive anything on two or four legs—inhabitants, oxen and donkeys, even fowl. Then Nefertiti's letter was delivered. Suppiluliumas had started the surprise raid in order to test the battle capacity of the Egyptian army at this time, after the death of the pharaoh. A letter such as this was the last message he expected to receive.

Of course the Hittite king, like every other head of government in the eastern world, had long believed that Queen Nefertiti had died years ago. For years nothing had been heard of her—and now this letter! Suppiluliumas suspected trickery at first. Surely the Egyptians intended for him to send one of his sons as husband to Nefertiti into the land on the Nile so that they could take him prisoner and kill him. Such a cheap revenge did not even require any military expenditure. What cowards these Egyptians were!

Suppiluliumas felt provoked and called in the great ones of his council. "Such a thing has never happened to me in my whole life," he said, clearly at a loss. Consulting with the wise men of his land, Suppiluliumas arrived at the conclusion that trickery can only be fought with trickery but that it was important to prevent any appearance of being irresolute. It was just possible that this completely incredible message from Queen Nefertiti was on the level after all.

Suppiluliumas therefore sent his chamberlain, Khattusaziti, on the road to Egypt. "Go and report to me true word, perhaps they wish to deceive me, perhaps they have a prince. You then report to me the true word."

Khattusaziti took on the suicide mission for his master. He had to be prepared to lose his head in Egypt if he uncovered a ruse. But Khattusaziti arrived in Akhetaten, realized Nefertiti's plight, and revealed himself as the ambassador of the king of the Hittites.

Nefertiti was thrown into deep despair by Suppiluliumas's suspicion. Time was growing short. A new pharaoh had to be found within ninety days because the pharaoh was buried ninety days after his death, and his successor was the one who had to perform the ritual opening of the mouth.

Ninety days is a scant thirteen weeks. It took a courier three weeks to travel from Khatti to Akhetaten. Now that six weeks had already passed—almost half the waiting period—the situation had not altered in any respect, and the leaders of the opposition lurked in the background. But it was especially in the ranks of the army that Nefertiti had powerful enemies. And then there was "god's father," Ay, whose influence must not be underrated. How was she to make all this clear to the king of the Hittites in faraway Khatti?

Nefertiti had exactly seven weeks left. If she sent another courier off immediately, and if he was not waylaid on the road or overtaken by a storm, and if the Hittite king sent off a son at once, and if...if...

It was the courage of desperation that bade Nefertiti to persevere. Her plan *must* succeed. Hastily she dictated a dispatch to Suppiluliumas.

Why did you say "they may deceive me" in that way? If I had a son, would I indeed write abroad to publish the distress of myself and my country? And as for you, you did not believe me and you have even spoken thus. He who was my husband is dead and I have no son. Never shall I take a servant of mine and marry him. Now I have written to no other country but only to you. Everyone believes that you have many sons, give me one in order that he may be my husband and reign in Egypt.

In this message too we sense between the lines the bitter pleading of this proud woman, though she was not prepared to put it directly into words. And once more we hear the idea so unacceptable to Nefertiti: "Never shall I take a servant of mine and marry him"—and thus make him the pharaoh.

The dispatch was taken by the messenger Hani. Apparently in company with Khattusaziti, he galloped off in the direction of Khatti. According to the records of Mursillis II, both reached Khatti—but King Suppiluliumas was not at home; he had set out in the meantime to conquer Karkhemish.

Situated on the right bank of the Euphrates, near what is today the city of Dsherabis, Karkhemish was an ancient city that existed as early as the third millenium B.C. and later became famous especially for the battle at which Nebuchadnezzar conquered the Egyptians in 606 B.C.

Suppiluliumas took Karkhemish in eight days and proclaimed his son Sarri Kusuh to be its king. Then he returned to Khatti, less in expectation of a reply from Nefertiti than from fear of the Anatolian winter, for by now late autumn had arrived.

Nefertiti had a scant four weeks left, and we can imagine that she counted the days. It was just as well she did not know what was going on in the Hittite capital during this time, for there a diplomatic duel was being fought, during which His Majesty Suppiluliumas did not mince words in his exchanges with Ambassador Hani. Hani, mindful of his mission, parried the verbal blows the Hittite dealt out to him. He simply must not return to Akhetaten without a prince.

More recent reconstructions of fragment finds from Suppiluliumas's annals render these conversations in great detail. While the Egyptian ambassador Hani was kept on tenterhooks, the Hittite king indulged in insults and reproaches.

> SUPPILULIUMAS: I myself was...friendly, but you, you suddenly did me evil. You came [?] and attacked the man [prince] of Kadesh whom I had taken away from the king of Hurri land. I, when I heard of this, became angry and sent forth my own troops and chariots and the lords. So they came and attacked your territory, the country of Amki. And when they attacked Amki, which is your country, you probably were afraid; [therefore] you keep asking for a son of mine [as if it were my] duty. He will in some way become a hostage, but king you will not make him.
>
> HANI: Oh, my lord, this is...our country's shame! If we had [a son of the king] at all, would we have come to a foreign country and kept asking for a lord for ourselves? Nibhururiya who was our lord died, a son he has not. Our lord's wife is solitary. We are seeking a son of our lord [Suppiluliumas] for the kingship in Egypt and for the woman our lady, we seek him as her husband! Further we went to no other country, only here did we come! Now, oh our lord, give us a son of thine!

It must have cost Hani considerable effort as the ambassador of the empire of Egypt to speak so subserviently to the Hittite king, even to plead with him. But in view of the desperate position of his queen, he gritted his teeth and did what was politically required.

For Nefertiti, these must have been the most difficult days of her life. These weeks would decide whether she would be able to win back the power that had been so ignominiously taken from her. But even more was at stake. If she could not find a husband, then the fate of the eighteenth dynasty, the most glorious in the history of Egypt, was sealed, as was the end of the Aten religion—and for Nefertiti the latter was at least equally terrible.

But King Suppiluliumas and the Egyptian ambassador Hani were still negotiating at the court of Khatti. By now Suppiluliumas had allowed himself to be persuaded that Nefertiti meant what she said. He made only one more demand. The old treaty of the Egyptians with the inhabitants of Kurustama was to be renewed. The people of Kurustama were Hittites and had once been raided by the Egyptians and carried off to the Nile. Subsequently the Hittites had made a treaty with the Egyptians which established that both peoples would leave each other in peace from then on.

Suppiluliumas had the treaty tablet put before him and the text confirmed by a codicil which the Egyptian ambassador had to sign. The codicil read: "Of old Khatti and Egypt were friendly with each other and now this, too, on our behalf has taken place between [them]. Thus Khatti and Egypt will be friendly with each other continuously." With this, all terms were met. Suppiluliumas chose Zannanza from among his sons to go to Egypt and marry Nefertiti. Then a Hittite would be the pharaoh.

Nefertiti knew nothing of this agreement—and the time

Pharaonic seals with cuneiform writing.

remaining had shrunk to a few days. Her sole comfort and support in this situation was her thirteen-year-old daughter, Ankhesenpaten. Mother and daughter discussed the matter for days on end, and through the nights, carefully considered all possibilities, and came to the conclusion that, for better or for worse, Nefertiti would have to marry an Egyptian, since no news had arrived from Khatti.

Perhaps the Hittite king had had the Egyptian ambassador killed. Such an event would be the cause of a major war between Egyptians and Hittites, since Suppiluliumas was only waiting for provocation. Nefertiti realized very clearly that only the Hittites could emerge victorious from such a struggle. It would mean the end of Egypt—and she must prevent that by any means, if necessary at the cost of her own person.

Nefertiti was still waiting for the Hittite prince. Hani had not yet returned from Khatti. And as long as he had not come back, there was a glimmer of hope.

However, Hani never returned. We know nothing of what happened to him. All we know is that he left Khatti with the happy news for Nefertiti that Prince Zannanza was on his way.

But Prince Zannanza never arrived in Akhetaten either. When he and his escort came to Syria and thus into Egyptian sovereign territory, "men and horses of Egypt" were lying in wait for him. Zannanza was treacherously murdered. Who the assassins were is still not clear. It may, of course, have been an accidental robbery and killing by some Bedouin tribe or other, but the suspicion is strong that the murder of the designated pharaoh had been engineered in cold blood by the Amun priests, the generals, or "god's father," Ay, who was eyeing the throne for himself.

As Mursillis II wrote in his "plague prayers," Suppiluliumas wept when he heard of the death of his son Zannanza, and he was overwhelmed by anger. It was clear to him that the Egyptian queen, famous not only for her beauty but also for her ingenuity, had tricked him. He, Suppiluliumas, king of the Hittites, had fallen into a trap set by a woman. Such deception was not to go unavenged.

News of the death of the Hittite prince Zannanza spread through Egypt like wildfire. Spellbound, the military leaders and officials looked northward in expectation of a retributive attack. When nothing happened for the present, the call for a new pharaoh grew louder.

Nefertiti had chosen a child to be king—a certain Tutankhaten, an eleven-year-old boy who had been raised in the northern palace of Akhetaten, although he was not Nefertiti's son. He was, however, related to her in some way—his origins are unexplained to this day—and he was the person Nefertiti wished to make pharaoh in her desperation to preserve the dynasty.

There are some Egyptologists, such as the American Edward Fay Campbell, who raise the question of whether the thirty-five-year-old queen might not have intended marrying Tutankhaten all along. We do know for a fact that he assumed his reign in Akhetaten. Wine-jar dockets list regnal years 1, 2, and 3. His wife, however, was not Nefertiti but her daughter, Ankhesenpaten.

Like her mother, Ankhesenpaten had been the secondary wife of a seriously ill pharaoh for barely two years before she herself ascended to the throne as great royal wife. At the age of thirteen Ankhesenpaten was two years older than King Tutankhaten, but she did not have the strong hand that could have guided the youthful king. Clearly Nefertiti had hoped to assume the role of counselor, and for the moment her plans were surely realized. But soon thereafter the queen had to admit that it was another who pulled the strings: the old "god's father," Ay. And behind Ay, the supreme commander of the cavalry, stood another high military official, a young man who was to attain power and renown later on: Horemheb, the supreme commander of the eastern armies.

The alliance of the two most important military officers in Egypt was dedicated to a very particular goal: removal of the Aten religion and revival of the traditional Amun cult. The eleven-year-old pharaoh, furnished with the insignia of unlimited power, was pulled back and forth between the advice of his mother-in-law, Nefertiti, who fought bitterly for the retention of the Aten faith, and the propaganda campaigns of old Ay, who preached the restitution of Amun. The pharaoh's wife, Ankhesenpaten, whom he loved dearly, took a kind of central position in the conflict. At the beginning of their reign Tutankhaten and Ankhesenpaten lived in the southern palace of Akhetaten, while Nefertiti went on inhabiting her palace at the northern limits of the town.

On the nineteenth day of 4 Akhet in the year 1346 Tutankhaten composed the text for a tall quartzite stela which is on exhibit in the Egyptian museum in Cairo today. This inscription, which clearly bears the spiritual signature of Horemheb, destroyed in a few sentences everything for which Nefertiti had fought all her life—the belief in the one god, the Aten, which had meant more to her than all the power on earth. The tall memorial stone reads as follows.

He [Tutankhaten] secured what had decayed among the monuments to the boundaries of eternity. He drove out what was sinful in all the land, while the truth remained in its place. He let the lie be an abomination in that the land is as it was in its primal time. But His Majesty climbed the throne as a king when the temples of the gods and goddesses from Elephantine to the marshes of the delta were about to be forgotten and their sanctuaries began to decay, becoming rubbish heaps, overgrown with weeds, and their holies of holies were as if they had never been, and their buildings a footpath. So the land experienced an illness and the gods neglected this land. If soldiers were sent to Syria to broaden the borders of Egypt, they brought about no success of any kind. If a god was implored to request something from him, he did not come; and if a goddess was approached, she did not come. Their hearts were weak in their bodies and they ceased to work.

It appears that the young Tutankhaten did not live long in Akhetaten; at least he did not consider Nefertiti's dream city as his principal residence, for a stela text from as early as Year 1 of his reign reports that His Majesty also spent some time on the estate of Thutmose I in Memphis, near the pyramids of Gizeh. It was here that Tutankhaten restored the old Amun cult. He had monumental images of the god cast from the finest gold from foreign countries and "enlarged all specifications for the temples, doubled, tripled, and quadrupled in silver, gold, lapis lazuli, turquoise, and all sorts of gems, royal linen, white linen, dishes, resin, fat, incense, perfumes, myrrh, without any limit to all good things."

Tutankhaten ordered the building of new Nile barges from Lebanese cedarwood, so as to furnish Amun once again with worthy vessels, such as had last been customary under Amunhotep III. New sculptures were also made for Ptah, the creator god of Memphis. The old temple estates, at one time rich sources of income for the priests, were assigned new slaves. The abandoned temple schools, where the clerical succession was recruited, once again opened their gates to the children of the aristocratic and the wealthy.

Nefertiti could not help but watch these events with anguish and sorrow. Akhetaten's palaces and temples emptied out, and the pitiful remnant of the faithful shrank steadily. As if the walls of the city had been attacked by leprosy, fear and disgust spread among the population of Akhetaten. As if the inhabitants were ashamed of the delusion that had caused them to worship the Aten, the only god, they moved away from the site of their shame. Tutankhaten set an example: together with his young wife,

Ankhesenpaten, he abandoned Akhetaten suddenly and forever, leaving the compounds of elegant buildings in what had once been the most beautiful city in the world to decay. This exodus happened between the third and fourth year of the pharaoh's reign, when he was about fourteen years old. Under pressure from his advisers, he and his wife changed their names—as once Akhenaten and Nefertiti had voluntarily done. The Aten was to be forgotten as quickly as possible, and Amun was to be raised to new glory. And so Tutankhaten and Ankhesenpaten became Tutankhamun and Ankhesenamun.

The young ruling couple returned to Thebes, and because no single find reports on a palace specific to the young pharaoh, scholars assume that Tutankhamun moved into the palace once occupied by Amunhotep III. Akhetaten, the magic name for a whole generation, fell into disrepute.

Only one person persisted in the old ways—Nefertiti. The queen was thirty-seven years old by now, still beautiful though somewhat aged. As recently as eight years before, she had been the most powerful woman in the world; now she was banished, despised, a woman of whom it was better not to speak. And if her name was mentioned at all, then only with the epithet "the heretic."

Where were all the men who had once prostrated themselves before her? What had become of her riches? What, finally, became of her? History is unable to give a definitive answer to any of these questions. Donald B. Redford and other leading Egyptologists argue that Nefertiti died shortly after Tutankhamun had left Akhetaten—that is, around the year 1344. Jar dockets in Nefertiti's palace, which go as high as year 3 of Tutankhamun's reign, support the hypothesis that Nefertiti died alone in a ghost town. Perhaps a terrible plague drove all the inhabitants from the city; then again, it may have been simply naked fear of the representatives of the counterreformation and the cruel military leaders backing Tutankhamun.

Nefertiti, in any case, never abandoned the city of her dreams. It was *her* city, *her* Akhetaten, *her* Horizon of the Sun. Here she had spent the few happy years of her eventful life; here she had laughed, loved, and suffered; and here she wanted to die. The Egypt of Tutankhamun—that was not *her* Egypt. The people who once again worshiped Amun, Ptah, and Osiris—they were not *her* people. They stood for a new old world, a world of appearances, of untruth and corruption—a world no longer Nefertiti's.

The Egyptian museum in Cairo has in its collections a plaster mask that was found in Amarna. Though the identity of its subject has not been definitively established, it is generally held to be Nefertiti's death mask. The right side of the face is damaged, but the characteristic cheekbones, somewhat prominent, and the slightly bulging forehead over the long, narrow eyebrows are nevertheless clearly recognizable. The eyes are more deep-set than we are used to seeing in other portraits of the queen, the lids are shut, the eyes are not defined. The mouth, far less curved than in the known busts, is closed. But it seems at the ready for a final word—which clearly was not spoken after all—and is smiling. The mouth bears a tenuous, secret smile, which we sense only if we tarry for a while in front of the relaxed face.

How can we explain the existence of this death mask? Is it possible that to the last the beautiful queen had the use of her entire court, complete with artists' workshops? Or was the same man at work here who had always been so fascinated by the timelessly beautiful features of the living woman—the master sculptor, Thutmose? There can be little doubt: the plaster impression carries his artistic signature. No Egyptian sculptor either before or after Thutmose achieved such perfection; never before or after Thutmose was such realism, such penetrating portraiture demanded; never before or after Thutmose was it conceivable that a queen would smile on her deathbed. This is a delicate, reserved smile, no longer touched by the hatred and strife that was to dominate Egypt in years to come.

EPILOGUE

The young Tutankhamun and his beautiful wife Ankhe-senamun were no more than puppets on the strings of the "vice-regent" Horemheb, "ambassador of the king to all the lands," "intimate of the special intimate of the king," and "true, much beloved scribe of the king," who set out to establish a military dictatorship in Egypt.

Tutankhamun did not die a natural death. In 1969, at the final X-ray examination of the mummy of this pharaoh who was roughly twenty at the time he died, Ronald Harrison discovered a hole in the back of the skull "which could have been caused by the blow of a cudgel or a sword hilt."

It was not Horemheb—as might have been expected—who next took the throne of the two lands, but the aged Ay. Was this a ruse on the part of the wily Horemheb? Was it his way of concealing his murderous intentions? Ay, old and feeble, assumed the office of pharaoh. At least, he

151

looked on the reign as an office. He merely represented royal prestige, and not a single memorable historical achievement is recorded for the period of his four-year rule. A ring with twin cartouches bearing the names of Ay and Ankhesenamun indicates that the aged Ay either married the young two-time widow or made her his co-regent. It is the last sign of life of Nefertiti's third daughter, whose fate was so similar to that of her mother.

If Ay took an indifferent or at least nonhostile stance toward the remnants of the waning Aten cult, a genuine iconoclasm toward the monuments of the recent past set in under the rule of Horemheb, who, at the urging of the Amun priesthood, ascended the throne after Ay's death. However, Horemheb was motivated less by religious fervor than by a craving for recognition. The self-anointed soldier-pharaoh had the works of art of his predecessors carried off; inscriptions were obliterated and his own name was set in their place. His actions did not distinguish between the heretic Akhenaten and the counterreformer Tutankhamun. In Karnak he demolished Nefertiti's great temple just as he did one built by Tutankhamun, using the components to build the great second pylon. He also realized a project that had been planned for ages—the powerful avenue of sphinxes between Luxor and Karnak. And always when he needed building materials, he shipped work crews down the Nile to Akhetaten, which lay abandoned, decayed, forgotten by most people.

The honorable soldier did not indulge himself in private escapades. Horemheb was married to one of Nefertiti's sisters, Mutnedjemet, of whom we know little. There are no preserved documents to clarify the relationship between the two sisters, but it is certain that Mutnedjemet was the younger of the two women. Portraits in the palace of Akhetaten frequently show her with Nefertiti's daughters or with two female dwarfs.

Horemheb, who reigned for almost thirty years, was the very opposite of a benevolent ruler. His penal code "to remove the cases of injustice in the land" was primarily directed against injustices that might be done to the pharaoh. Horemheb wished it known that tax evasion—a taxable steer hide, for example—would be punished "with 100 blows and five bleeding wounds." Unscrupulously the soldier-pharaoh plundered tombs, nor did he stop at the final resting place of his predecessor, Ay. It has remained a mystery to this day why he left the tomb of Tutankhamun unmolested, though it was full to bursting with priceless treasures.

Horemheb was apparently ignorant of where Nefertiti lay buried. According to present-day scholarship, Nefertiti was not laid to rest in any of the Amarna tombs excavated so far. But we may assume that so devout, so intelligent a woman as the beautiful queen made provisions for her life in the hereafter. And of course there are always new rumors and speculations regarding Nefertiti's final resting-place. Around Amarna, for example, the fellahin tell the tale of one night during the 1880s, when a column of muffled figures, working by torchlight, carried off a sarcophagus on their shoulders....

We only know as fact that, soon afterward, jewelry from the eighteenth dynasty and rings bearing Nefertiti's name cartouche were offered for sale in Cairo. Today they are preserved in various European museums. There is no trace of Nefertiti's sarcophagus or of her mummy.

Appendixes

APPENDIX A
Partial Chronology
of the New Kingdom
(after Erik Hornung)

	Established Dates	*Probable Dates*
Ahmose	1559/45–1534/24	spring 1552–summer 1527
Amunhotep I	1534/24–1514/04	summer 1527–March 22, 1506
Thutmose I	1514/04–1501/1491	March 23, 1506–September 1494
Thutmose II	1501/1491–1490	December 1494–June 1491
Hatshepsut	May 1, 1490–1469/68	May 1, 1490–December 1469
Thutmose III	May 1, 1490–March 14, 1438	May 1, 1490–fall 1438
Amunhotep II	November 16, 1438–1412/11	November 16, 1438–January 30, 1412
Thutmose IV	1412/11–1405/02	September 1412–early 1402
Amunhotep III	1405/02–1367/63	June 7, 1402–August 1364
Amunhotep IV (Akhenaten)	1367/63–1351/45	August 1364–February 1347
Smenkhkare		early 1351–late 1348
Tutankhaten (Tutankhamun)	1351/45–1342/36	February 1347–early 1338
Ay	1342/36–1337/31	early 1338–1334
Horemheb	1337/31–1307/10	1334–late 1306

155

APPENDIX B
Nefertiti's Egyptian Family Relationships

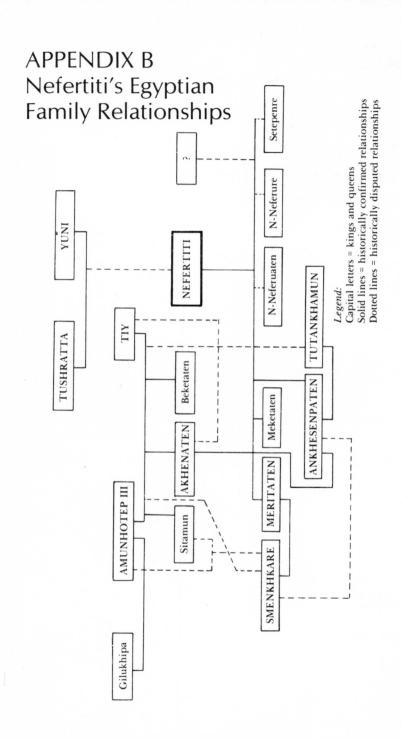

Legend:
Capital letters = kings and queens
Solid lines = historically confirmed relationships
Dotted lines = historically disputed relationships

APPENDIX C
Chronology of Nefertiti's Life

Age	Regnal Year		Year	
1–14			1381/ 67	Childhood and adolescence at the court of Tushratta in Mitanni.
15	36		1366	Marriage to Amunhotep III.
16	37		1365	Secondary wife at the court of Amunhotep III in Malkata (Thebes).
17	38	Akhenaten	1364	Widowed by the death of Amunhotep III.
18	1		1363	Marriage to Amunhotep IV, residing in Malkata.
19	2		1362	Birth of first daughter, Meritaten.
20	3		1361	Birth of second daughter, Meketaten.
21	4		1360	Birth of third daughter, Ankhesenpaten; decision to found Akhetaten.
22	5		1359	
23	6	Amunhotep III	1358	Inspects building site (Day 13, Fourth Peret). Move to Akhetaten; birth of fourth daughter, Neferneferuaten.
24	7		1357	In residence in Akhetaten with Akhenaten. Late: official dedication.
25	8		1356	Presumptive creation of the bust of Nefertiti.
26	9		1355	Completion of all temples and palaces of Akhenaten. Birth of fifth daughter, Neferneferure.

27	10	1354	
28	11	1353	Birth of sixth daughter, Setepenre.
29	12	1352	Acceptance of tribute in the temple of the Aten, November 21.
			Last portrait together with Akhenaten and the six daughters.
			Death of Meketaten.
30	13	1351	Beginning of her star's sinking.
			Marriage of Meritaten and Smenkhkare.
			Smenkhkare "the darling of Akhenaten."
31	1/14	1350	Rejection of the title great royal wife.
			Meritaten becomes the "First Lady"; Smenkhkare made co-regent.
32	2/15	1349	Final break with Akhenaten.
			Smenkhkare given Nefertiti's epithet of Neferneferuaten.
			Nefertiti living in the northern palace.
33	3/16	1348	Marriage of Ankhesenpaten (age 12) to her father, Akhenaten.
34	4/17	1347	Death of Smenkhkare, followed shortly by that of Akhenaten.
			Nefertiti's letter to Suppiluliumas.
35	1	1346	Marriage of Tutankhaten to Ankhesenpaten, who governs in Akhetaten.
36	2	1345	Nefertiti, forgotten, living on in the northern palace of Akhetaten.
37	3	1344	Abandonment of Akhetaten by Tutankhamun. Death of Nefertiti (according to Redford).

Smenkhkare (spanning rows 32–34)

Tutankhamun (spanning rows 36–37)

APPENDIX D
The Egyptian Calendar

There were only three seasons of four months each in ancient Egypt: Akhet (the time of flooding), Peret (the time of sowing), and Shemu (the time of harvest).

MONTHS	*Akhet* June 15–October 15	*Peret* October 15–February 15	*Shemu* February 15–June 15
1	Thot June 15–July 15	Tybi October 15– November 15	Pakhons February 15– March 15
2	Paophi July 15– August 15	Mekhir November 15– December 15	Payni March 15– April 15
3	Athyr August 15– September 15	Phamenat December 15– January 15	Epiphi April 15– May 15
4	Khoyak September 15– October 15	Pharmuti January 15– February 15	Mesore May 15– June 15

Suggested Reading

Aldred, Cyril, *Akhenaten and Nefertiti*. New York: Viking Press, 1973.

———, *Egypt to the End of the Old Kingdom*. London: Thames and Hudson, 1965.

Bille-de Mot, Eléonore, *The Age of Akhenaten* (tr. by Jack Lindsay). London: Evelyn, A & M, 1968.

Campbell, Edward Fay, *The Chronology of the Amarna Letters*. Baltimore: Johns Hopkins University Press, 1964.

———, *The Lost Pharaohs*. New York: Holt, Rinehart and Winston, 1961.

Cottrell, Leonard, *The Anvil of Civilization*. London: Faber, 1958.

Davies, Norman de Garis, *The Tomb of Two Sculptors at Thebes*. New York: Metropolitan Museum, 1925.

Desroches-Noblecourt, Christiane, *Tutankhamen*. London: Connoisseur, 1963.

Erman, Adolf, *Life in Ancient Egypt*. London: Macmillan, 1894.

Fairservis, Walter A., Jr., *Ancient Kingdoms of the Nile*. New York: Thomas Y. Crowell Co., 1962.

Gardiner, Alan H., *Egypt of the Pharaohs*. London: Oxford University Press, 1961.

Giles, Frederick John, *Ikhnaton: Legend and History*. Cranbury, N.J.: Fairleigh Dickinson University Press, 1972. London: Hutchinson, 1972.

Grayson, A. K., and Donald B. Redford, *Papyrus and Tablet*. Hemel Hempstead: Prentice-Hall, 1973.

Harris, James E., and Kent R. Weeks, *X-Raying the Pharaohs* London: Macdonald & Jane's, 1973.

Mercer, Samuel A. B., *The Tell el-Amarna Tablets*. Toronto: The Macmillan Company of Canada, 1939.

Neubert, Otto, *Valley of the Kings*. London: Robert Hale, 1957.

Peet, Thomas E., *Akhenaten, Ty, Nefertete and Metnezemt.* Liverpool: Liverpool University Press, 1923.

Pendlebury, John D. S., *Tell el-Amarna.* Toronto: The Macmillan Company of Canada, 1935.

Redford, Donald B., *Studies in the History and Chronology of the Eighteenth Egyptian Dynasty.* Oxford: O.U.P., 1968.

Riefstahl, Elizabeth, *Thebes in the Time of Amunhotep III.* Norman, Okla.: University of Oklahoma Press, 1964.

Samson, Julia, *Amarna, City of Akhenaten and Nefertiti.* Warminster, Wilts.: Aris & Phillips, 1972.

Silverberg, Robert, *Akhnaten, the Rebel Pharaoh.* Philadelphia: Chilton Books, 1964.

Vandenberg, Philipp, *The Curse of the Pharaohs.* London: Hodder & Stoughton, 1976.

Velikovsky, Immanuel, *Oedipus and Akhnaton: Myth and History.* London: Sidgwick & Jackson, 1960.

Wells, Evelyn, *Nefertiti.* Garden City, N.Y.: Doubleday & Co., 1964.

White, J. E. Manchip, *Ancient Egypt.* New York: Thomas Y. Crowell Co., 1952.